I0221905

James Gopsil's Sons

Gopsill's Street Guide of Philadelphia

James Gopsil´s Sons

Gopsill's Street Guide of Philadelphia

ISBN/EAN: 9783337020415

Printed in Europe, USA, Canada, Australia, Japan

Cover: Foto ©Andreas Hilbeck / pixelio.de

More available books at **www.hansebooks.com**

THE ONLY AUTHENTIC AND RELIABLE STREET GUIDE OF
PHILADELPHIA PUBLISHED.

GOPSILL'S

STREET GUIDE

OF

PHILADELPHIA.

𝕻ocket 𝕰dition.

PHILADELPHIA:

JAMES GOPSILL'S SONS, PUBLISHERS,

No. 518 WALNUT STREET.

Entered according to Act of Congress in the year 1898, by
JAMES GOPSILL'S SONS,
in the office of the Librarian of Congress, at Washington, D. C.

NOTICE.

THE publishers in presenting this Guide to the public do so with the assurance that it is the most complete and accurate Street Guide of Philadelphia yet issued. A thorough and systematic canvass of the entire city has been made and verified at the office of the City Survey Department. No time or expense has been spared to make the Guide thoroughly reliable.

There are a number of alleged Street Guides published which have been pirated from our former Guides and Directories, and foisted on a confiding public from year to year as original, official, and copyrighted. It is the intention of the publishers to prosecute any infringement of this work.

JAMES GOPSILL'S SONS,
Publishers.

SHRIVER, BARTLETT & CO. {ADJUSTMENTS COLLECTIONS

GOPSILL'S

STREET GUIDE

OF THE CITY OF PHILADELPHIA.

☞ For KEY TO STREET NAMES, see page 21.

☞ By the decimal system of numbering streets adopted in this city, one hundred numbers are allotted to each square, commencing at the DELAWARE, running WEST, and at MARKET, running NORTH and SOUTH. All other streets not commencing at either the above points are numbered in accordance with this system.

☞ All parallel streets running North and South will be found under N and S, as N Front, S Front, N Darien, S Darien. On parallel streets E and W of Front, E is given as the distinction, as Girard Avenue, and E Girard Avenue, Norris and E Norris; in Germantown, Gtn av is the dividing line.

ABBREVIATIONS.—ab, *above*; al, *alley*; av, *avenue*; Bdg, *Bridesburg*; cem, *cemetery*; Bln, *Bustleton*; B Town, *Branch Town*; C Grove, *Cedar Grove*; C Hill, *Chestnut Hill*; ct, *court*; C'ville, *Collegeville*; Cr'ville, *Crescentville*; Del, *Delaware*; E, *east*; Falls, *Falls of Schuylkill*; F'ville, *Feltonville*; Fkd, *Frankford*; fr, *from*; Gtn, *Germantown*; Hbg, *Holmesburg*; H'ville, *Hestonville*; Ktn, *Kensington*; la, *lane*; Myk, *Manayunk*; M'ville, *Mechanicsville*; M'Town, *Milestown*; Montg'y, *Montgomery*; Mt Vernon, *Mount Vernon*; n, *near*; N Town, *Nicetown*; N, *north*; opp, *opposite*; P'ville, *Paschalville*; pl, *place*; R Sun, *Rising Sun*; riv, *River*; rd, *road*; Schy'l, *Schuylkill*; S'ville, *Somerville*; S, *south*; Spg Garden, *Spring Garden*; sq, *square*; Susq'ana av, *Susquehanna av*; ter, *terrace*; W, *West*; W P, *West Philadelphia*; W Hall, *White Hall*; Wiss, *Wissahickon*.

CHANGES IN THE NAMES OF STREETS.

GIVING OLD AND NEW NAMES.

Approved by BOARD OF SURVEYORS, February 23, 1897. Under ORDINANCE OF COUNCILS, December 27, 1895, and revised in accordance with ORDINANCE OF COUNCILS, and approved July 16, 1897.

Aberdeen now S American
Academy now Appletree
Ackley (W P) now St. Bernard
Acorn al now S Schell
Adams (Fkd) now Adams av
Adams (Gtn) now McCallum
Adams (Myk) now Harvey
Adams (W P) now Stiles
Adelena now E Lippincott
Adelhe (W P) now Upland
Adelphi now St James
Adelphia al now N Hancock
Adrian (Jefferson E of N Front) row N Lee
Adrian (N fr Otter) now N Lee
Adrian (Feltonville) now Lee
Adrian (Wiss) now Lauriston
Afton now Aikin

Agnes now S Alder
Airy now E Harold
Airy (Myk) now Boone
Alaska now Eater
Albemarle (S 28th, N of Ellsworth) now Peters
Albert (1024 S 12th) now League
Albion now N & S Van Pelt
Albrecht now Colona
Alexander now S Marshall
Alexander av (E & W) (S Clarion, S of Federal) now Latona
Alexander av (N & S) now S Juniper
Alford now Addison
Allen (Fkd) now Overington
Allison (Reed, W of S 9th) now S Percy

RICHARDSON & ROSS, 30th & Race Sts.

Allison av (Myk) now Wendover
Allison pl now Appletree
Allman (W P) now Regent
Almond (717 S 2d) now Kenilworth
Alroy now Lemon
Altmaier now Fontain
Aman (Dickinson to S. 12th) now Gerritt
Amboy now N Clarion
Ameaseka (W P) now Beaumont
Amity now Burns
Anderson now Gratz
Andress now N Camac
Andrew now E Lippincott
Angle (R Sun) now Atlantic
Anita now Annin
Ann (S fr 2649 Ktn av), now Oakdale
Ann (W fr 264 S 17th), now Manning
Ann (Fkd), now Granite
Ann (Myk) now Eva
Ann (W P) now N & S 71st
Anna (fr Hart la) now Braddock
Anna, now Eyre
Annapolis, now S Hancock
Ansbury av now N Howard
Anthony, now S Beulah
Anthracite now Albert
Aramingo, now E Letterly
Arcadia, now Coral
Ardleigh av (Gtn), now Sullivan
Argyle, now Tree
Arizona (S of Walnut), now Latimer
Arizona (W P) now St. James
Ark now French
Arrison ct now Ionic
Ash (825 Richmond) now Fleicher
Ash (Mercer, N of Susq'ana av) now E Fletcher
Ashburton (W P) now Waverly
Ashbury now S Randolph
Ashford now Spring
Ashhurst now S Bodine
Ashland now S Warnock
Ashland (Myk), now Lauriston
Ashland av (W P), now Thole
Aspen (Chancellor, W of S 8th) now S Schell
Aspen st pl now Waverly
Aster (Gtn) now N Franklin
Asylum (S Broad, S of Spruce) now De Lancey
Asylum av now S Rosewood
Asylum pl now Fulton
Atherton now S Fairhill
Athol now Reach
Atlanta (W P), now Olive
Atlantic av now N Smedley

Atmore now Reno
Aubrey pl now N Clarion
Auburn now Kimball
Augusta pl now Spring
Aurora now Latimer
Austin now S Alder
Autumn (S fr Ranstead), now S Uber
Autumn (S fr Vine) now N Bouvier
Baily now Emily
Baird (Gtn) now Newhall
Baker (S Marshall to S 8th) now Pemberton
Baker (N Town), now Kerbaugh
Balch now N Philip
Baldwin (Tac) now Higbee
Baltic pl now S American
Baltimore now S Sydenham
Bambrey now Reno
Banana now Walter
Bancroft (Mifflin to McKean) now S Alder
Bancroft (N fr Dauphin to York) now N Smedley
Bangor now Pemberton
Bankers' ct (W P) now Union
Bankson now Park av
Barclay (676 N Broad) now Melon
Barclay (320 S 6th) now De Lancey
Barcroft av now S Alder
Barker now Ludlow
Barley now Waverly
Barlow (Reed to Wharton, W of S 5th) now S Reese
Barlow (N fr Pemberton, W of S 7th) now S Perth
Barnett now Alter
Barnewell now S Taney
Barney av now N Croskey av
Barr now Lycoming
Barron (Gaskill to South) now S American
Barrow now S Orianna
Barton now N Warnock
Bartram now N Woodstock
Bateman now S Opal
Baton (McKean, W of S 19th) now S Opal
Baton (Bainbridge, W of S 7th) now S Perth
Bay now Cypress
Bayard now Earp
Beach (W P) now Ionic
Beaver now Wildey
Becket now Melon
Beckwith now S Sartain
Beechwood (Pittville) now Ferdinand

RICHARDSON & ROSS, 30th & Race Sts.

Belair (Myk) now Dexter
Belgrade pl now E George
Bellevue (N 20th to N 22d) now Wensley
Bellevue (Had) now Summer
Belrose now N Bodine
Benezet now Cuthbert
Benners ct (2339 N 26th) now Nevada
Bennett now Ionic
Benton now S Hicks
Bergdoll Ter now Newkirk
Berlin now S Leithgow
Bertha now Letterly
Bethlehem now Helen
Bevan now Livingston
Bexley (Gtn) now Laurens
Bicking (W P) now Yocum
Bickley (Olney) now Palethorp
Biddle now Buttonwood
Bingham's ct now S Orianna
Birch (W fr N 8th, N of Arch) now Appletree
Birch (1512 Fitzwater) now S Hicks
Bishop now Silver
Bismarck now S Mildred
Blackburn now S Alder
Bland now S Garnet
Bley now Coral
Blight now S Watts
Blodgett now N De Kalb
Bloyd (Gtn) now Grange
Bockius (Gtn) now Devon
Bohemia pl now Fulton
Bolton now E Schiller
Bolton (Myk) now Ripka
Bond (S 9th bel Spruce) now Cypress
Bonner pl now Hope
Boone (1412 Howard) now Gerritt
Bordeau av (N & S) now N Wendle
Borden now Earp
Borie av now Pacific
Boston av now Boston
Boudinot (Ontario to Tioga) now Arbor
Bower (E fr Trenton av) now E Hewson
Bowman (Gtn) now Stafford
Bowser (Fkd) now Plum
Boyd's av now N Warnock
Boyer pl now De Gray
Bradford (Spruce, W of S 16th) now S Smedley
Bradford (S Alder, S of South) now Kater
Branch (224 N 3d) now Florist
Branch (Gtn) now N Bouvier
Branch av now Titan

Branners al now N Reese
Bridge (Falls) now Calumet
Brier pl now S Alder
Bright (2233 Auburn) now Janney
Brighton now Chancellor
Brinkley pl now N Marshall
Brinton (435 Master) now N Orkney
Brinton (923 S 8th) now Hall
Brinton (710 S 12th) now Kenilworth
Brogan Low Irving
Brook now N Bodine
Brown (Wakeling, S E of E Thompson) now Edgemont
Brown's ct now Shamokin
Bruster now Day
Buckley now Cypress
Budd (308 S 12th) now Cypress
Budd (Hbg) now Tackawanna
Buddens al now Appletree
Burd now S Hancock
Burmont now Elsinore
Burnett now S 26th
Burton now Naudain
Butler's av (S Juniper, S of Spruce) now Panama
Butler pl (N fr Panama) now S Clarion
Butler pl (Sansom, W of S 10th) now S Alder
Byron now E Lippincott
Cabot (Lehigh av, N E of E Thompson) now Mercer
Cadwallader (1412 Fitzwater) now S Rosewood
Caldwell (912 N 13th) now George
Caldwell (207 S 24th) now Chancellor
Camelia now Sepviva
Camilla now Kimball
Campbell (S Randolph to S 6th) now Fulton
Campbell (Fitzwater to Fulton, W of S 5th) now S Randolph
Canal (Cambridge to N American) now N Bodine
Canal (N 2d to N American) now Laurel
Canal (Gtn av to Laurel) now N Hancock
Canal (Fkd av to Gtn av) now Allen
Canal (N Lawrence W of N 4th) now N Orkney
Canal (Miller, S of E Lehigh av) now E Oakdale
Canal (Moyam'g av to 5th & S 13th to Juniper) now Sigel
Canby now St James

SHEET ASPHALT PAVING of all kinds.

Canova (W P) now Frazier
Canton now N Percy
Capewell now E Fletcher
Carbon (1916 South), now S Alder
Carman now N Perth
Carolina pl now S Alder
Caroline (N fr Dauphin) now Myrtle-
  wood
Caroline (420 Wharton) now S Law-
  rence
Carrie (Bdg) now Cooper
Carters' al now Ionic
Carver now Rodman
Cass now Cabot
Castle st ct now N Clifton
Cathedral av (W P) now Stiles
Cattell (W P) now Malvern
Cavin now N Opal
Cedar (Myk) now Jamestown
Cedar la (Gtn) (fr Haines to Chew)
  now Bellfield
Cedar la (Gtn) (Walnut to Haines)
  now Magnolia
Cedar la (Gtn) (Musgrave to
  Church la) now Musgrave
Cemetery (Myk) now Conarroe
Centennial Av (1813 Jefferson) now
  Gratz
Centre (Gtn) now Rittenhouse
Centre (Myk) now Dupont
Centre (W P) now Cuthbert
Centre (W P) (Sloan to State) now
  Willow
Centre (W P) (Westminster av to
  Parrish) now Wiota
Ceruse (Addison to Waverly) now S
  Hicks
Ceruse (Waverly to Lombard) now
  S Sydenham
Chalfont av (W P) now N Napa
Chalkley Hall la now Sepviva
Chancery la now Mascher
Chant now Ludlow
Chapel (Angora) now Redfield
Chapman now St Albans
Charles (406 South) now S Leith-
  gow
Charles (610 Wash'n av) now S
  Marshall
Charles (Fkd) now August
Charles (Myk) now Markle
Charles ter (W P) now Walden
Charlesee av now Wilt
Charlotte now N Orianna
Charter now E Dakota
Chase pl now Judson
Chatham (519 Buttonwood) now N
  Randolph
Chauncey now Cleveland

Chelsea (W P) now Summer
Cherry (Fkd) now Hawthorne
Cherry (K Sun) now N Camac
Cherry la (Gtn) now Weaver
Chester now N Darien
Chestnut (Myk) N E fr 4413 Main
  now Baker
Chestnut av (Bln) now Corinthian
Chestnut pl (W P) now Grove
China (415 Buttonwood) now N Law-
  rence
China (1002 S Front) now Alter
Chippewa now S 27th
Chubb now S Mildred
Church (N Stillman to N 25th) now
  Ralston
Church (fr Taney) now Stiles
Church (Park drive to Ridge av)
  now Weightman
Church (Bdg) now Pratt
Church (Gtn) now Phil-Ellena
Church (Hbg) now Charles
Church (Myk) now Krams
Church (W P) now Walden
Church av now S Opal
Citron now North
Clairmont (W P) now Melon
Clara now N Colorado
Clare now S Fairhill
Clarence now Sergeant
Clarion (N fr Elkhart) now Brad-
  dock
Clark (S 3d, S of Carpenter) now
  League
Clark (Bdg) now Livingston
Clark (Hbg) now Fuller
Clay (Myk) now Boone
Clay (S 20th, S of Spruce) now
  Panama
Claymont now N Lambert
Clayton now Meredith
Clement now S Chadwick
Cleveland av (W P) now Univer-
  sity
Clifford (Fkd) now Rupert
Clifford's al now Filbert
Clifton (South to Bainbridge) now
  S Clifton
Clifton (2715 Neff) now Tilton
Clifton (Gtn) now E Garfield
Clinton (N Town) now Elser
Clinton (Olney) now Mascher
Clothier now Victoria
Clover now Ranstead
Clyde pl now N Reese
Cobb now S Lawrence
Coburn now S Philip
Coffman now Seltzer

RICHARDSON & ROSS, 30th & Race Sts.

CLAIMS AND LITIGATED MATTERS.

Colebrook pl now Clymer
Coleman now S Beechwood
Collar now E Wilt
Collard now Cooper
Collingwood Low Elkhart
Columbus now E Elkhart
Colville now N Lee
Comlyn (Gtn) now Bringhurst
Commerce, N (W fr 2637 E York) now Moyer
Como (N 8th, N of Cambria) now Birch
Como (N 11th, N of Cambria) now Orleans
Compromise now Cypress
Comptroller now S Philip
Concord now Fulton
Congress now Pemberton
Connecticut av now Newkirk
Conroy now McClellan
Continental av now Aspen
Cook (1625 Pine) now S Chadwick
Cooke (1817 Tulip) now E Wilt
Coombes now Cuthbert
Cooper (N fr Ontario), now Palethorp
Cooper (W fr S 20th), now St James
Cope (E fr Amber), now E Lippincott
Cope (S fr 2312 Ionic) now S Bonsall
Copia now Webster
Corn now S American
Corr (N fr N Smedley) now Victoria
Corr (B Town) now N Cleveland
Corson (C Hill) now Sullivan
Costello (Gtn) now Nedro
Cottage now Sigel
Coulston now Edgeley
Court (S fr Brown, E of N Front) now N Lee
Court now Olive
Courtland (Fkd) now Rauch
Cowley now Winter
Cox now Commerce
Craig's pl now Chancellor
Cranson now S Schell
Craven now Florist
Crawford now Freedley
Crease's la (Roxb) now Livezey
Cresson (148 N 5th) now Quarry
Crockett's ct now Ranstead
Crosby now S Phillip
Cross (Naudain to Rodman) now S Franklin
Crown now N Lawrence
Crumbach now Gerritt
Cuba now S Orianna
Cullen now Naudain

Culvert (E fr Jasper, N of Allegheny av) now E Willard
Culvert (Fkd) now Imogene
Cumberland (Gtn) now Lena
Curlew (W P) now Sloan
Curran pl (623 N 4th) now Potts
Curren pl now N Orianna
Custer av (P'ville) now Cranmer
Cuyler now Shamokin

Dana now Nectarine
Darcy now Kenilworth
Darwin (N Town) now St Lukes
Davenport now Manning
Davis (2210 N Howard) now Colona
Davis (1210 N 12th) now Walter
Davis (N Town) now Henvis
Davis Landing, now Fitzwater
Daymon (Falls) now N Shedwick
Deacon now N Jessup
Deal now E Eyre
Dean (N fr Porter) now S Iseminger
Dean (1214 Walnut) now S Camac
Decatur now S Marshall
Deimling pl now S Bodine
De Kalb sq (W P) now S De Kalb
Delaware now Madison
Delaware av (Hbg) now Rhawn
Denmark now Fernon
Denver now E Auburn
Depot now Brandywine
Deshong now Annin
Devon (S of Federal, W of S 23d) now S Bucknell
Devon (Gtn) now Nelson
Dewees (N Town) now Fowler
Diamond (1229 Fitzwater) S Iseminger
Dickinson (2525 Collins) now Firth
Dillmore now S Percy
Dillwyn now N Orianna
D'Invillier (W P) now N 47th
Division (N W fr Richmond) now E Clementine
Division (Myk) (Cinnaminson to Hermitage) now Mansion
Division (Myk) (Main to Cresson) now Conarroe
Dixey now S Woodstock
Donk now S Mole
Dobbins now Cypress
Dodia now S Bambrey
Dohan (W P) now Reno
Donald now McClellan
Donath (Gtn) now Tacoma
Donneganna now Latona
Donnelly (Salter to Montrose) now S Clifton

ASPHALTUM BLOCKS and TILES.

Donnelly (fr Christian to Montrose) now S Darien
Dott (N fr Jefferson) now N Lambert
Dorsey now Waverly
Dorsey (W P) now Filbert
Douglass (Gtn) now Cosgrove
Dover pl now Rodman
Doyle now Rodman
Drayton now Titan
Drexel (Fkd) now Tackawanna
Drinker now Quarry
Drums av now N Mildred
Duane now N Camac
Dubree (Vineyard to Wylie) now Cameron
Dugan now S Hicks
Dunlap now S Croskey
Duponceau now S Darien
Durham pl now N Fairhill
Dutton (90 Morris) now S Lee
Dutton (E fr S 5th) now Addison
Dutton (Gtn) now N Woodstock
Duval (Wayne to Sherman, Gtn) now Pomona
Duval (W P) now Moravian
Dyson (W P) now N May
Eagle ct now Irving
Eaglefield (W P) now Cambridge
Eagleson now Montrose
Eakin now S Clifton
Earp now Nectarine
E Canal (N Front to Fkd av) now E Allen
E Tremont now William
Eberle (Gtn) now N Lambert
Edgeley (Marston to N 27th) now French
Edgeley (W P) (Belmont av to N 38th) now Midvale
Edward (Fkd) now Elwyn
Edward (W P) now Natrona
Effingham now S Marshall
Elder now N Clifton
Eleven Mile la (Hbg) now Linden
Elfreth's al now Cherry
Eliza now Ingersoll
Elizabeth (2619 Ktn av) now E Harold
Elizabeth (Falls) now Cresswell
Ella now E Arizona
Ellwood now Page
Ellwood av (Oak la) now N Fairhill
Elm (N fr Ann, W of Bath) now Cooper
Elm (N W fr Wildey) now Earl
Elm av (W P) now Parkside av
Elm pl now St. James

Elmslie's al now St James
Elwyn now N Hutchinson
Ely av now Reno
Emeline (E fr Trenton av) now Martha
Emeline (W fr 618 S 8th) now Kater
Emerson (Hbg) now De Victor
Emlen (Trenton av to E Thompson) now E Boston
Emlen (N 7th to N 8th) now Boston
Emma (E Susq'anna av, S of Amber) now Martha
Emma (E Lippincott, E of N Front) now N Water
Emmet now S Orianna
Emmet (W fr 1312 S 3d) now Sears
Emmet (N fr 2723 Thompson) now Pennock
Emory now E Sergeant
Eneu now Latona
Engle (Gtn) now Osceola
Engleside av now Bailey
Engleside pl now Turner
English now S Reese
Enquirer now N Marvine
Enterprise now Greenwich
Erety now St James
Ericsson (S Percy to S 9th) now Salter
Ericsson (Salter to Montrose) now S Percy
Erie now S Warnock
Ernst now S Delhi
Esher now Marston
Espey now S Park av
Essex now S Mildred
Eustis now McClellan
Euston av now Stella
Eutaw now N Franklin
Evangelist now Fulton
Evans (fr Clearfield) now Collins
Evans (N fr 2215 Summer) now N Croskey
Evans (fr Ellsworth, W of S 2d) now S Bodine
Evans (Falls) now Powers
Evans (Gtn) now Lena
Evelina now Locust
Everett now Montrose
Everett pl now Hope
Evergreen row St Albans
Exchange pl now S American
Exeter now Ionic
Ezekiel (Myk) now Boone
F (244 S 22d) row Rittenhouse sq
Faas pl now N Clifton
Factory now DeLancey
Fair (Myk) now Lalg

RICHARDSON & ROSS, 30th & Race Sts.

EQUITABLE RATES—PROMPT RETURNS.

Fairfax av (Gtn) now Wakefield
Fairfield now Commerce
Fairview av (Falls) now Ainslie
Fairview av (P'ville) now Harley
Fallon now S Darien
Falls rd now Conshohocken
Far'es ct now Summer
Farragut ter (W P) now S Markoe
Farrell now S Warnock
Farson pl new Sarah
Faulkner now S Orianna
Fawn (fr 613 Ann) now S Sheridan
Fayette (N fr 925 Filbert) now N Hutchinson
Fayette (N Town) now Luzerne
Fell now Morse
Fern (Gtn) now Laurens
Fetter's la now Cherry
Field now Emily
Fillmore (N fr 2500 Ktn av) now A
Fillmore (S fr DeLancey) now S Bouvier
Filson now N Croskey
Fishbourne pl now S Sheridan
Fisher (2735 E Cumberland) now Emery
Fisher (S 6th to S 7th) now Fernon
Fisher's av (W P) now Vogdes
Fitler now Tilghman
Fleeson (Myk) now Delmar
Fleet now S Randolph
Fleetwood av now N Jessup
Fleming (W fr Capitol) now Urhanna
Florence (N fr North) now N Bouvier
Florence (S fr 1030 Montrose) now S Clifton
Florida now S Marvine
Flower now Olive
Forbes now S Bambrey
Ford now S Uber
Foster (W P) now Cuthbert
Fothergill now S Hutchinson
Fowler now N Chadwick
Fox (N 12th to N Sydenham) now Hazzard
Fox (S E fr Collins) now E Hazzard
Fox (E Cumberland, E of N Front) now N Water
Fox (N Town) now N Hicks
Fox's ct (1221 South) now S Fawn
Fraley's al now Melvale
Francis (1114 S 12th) now Alter
Franklin (W fr S 23d) now Cypress
Franklin (Bdg) now Brill
Franklin (Gtn) now Hortter

Franklin (N Town) now Dell
Franklin Cemetery av now E Elkhart
Frederick (W fr S 30th) now McClellan
Frederick (Berks to Montg'y av) now N Clifton
Freedley now N Cleveland
Fremont (W fr 2840 Salmon) now E Auburn
Fremont (2828 N 12th) now E William
Freytag al now S Reese
Fricke (Gtn) now Cornelius
Fried's av now N Perth
Friedlander now N Woodstock
Fulmer (W P) now Chelwynde
Fulton (S fr 2208 Race), now N Croskey
Fulton (W fr 746 S 12th) now St Albans
Fulton (W fr Tulip) now E Rush
Funk (Tac) now Howell
G (S 22d, S of Walnut) now Latimer
Gaffney's av now S Sheridan
Gallatin pl now S Howard
Galloway now Manton
Gampher's av now S Reese
Garden now N Darien
Garden (W P) now Budd
Garibaldi (R Sun) now Thayer
Garnet (N fr P & R Rw to Hart la) now Ruth
Garside row N Bonsall
Gatzmer now Bright
Geary (Ginnodo to Francis) now Leland
Gebhard now N Mole
Geisler now E Elkhart
Geiss now Collins
George (Bdg) now Belgrade
Gerhard now S Sartain
Gerker now Livingston
German now Fitzwater
Getz row S Jessup
Gilbert now Olive
Giles now Nicholas
Gillingham now Stiles
Gillis al now S Reese
Glenwood now N Hancock
Godey now S Sheridan
Godfrey (Moyam'g av, S of Tasker) now Fernon
Godfrey av now N Leithgow
Gold (Judson to N 23d) now Brandywine
Gold (N E fr 2327 Penna av) now Judson

SHEET ASPHALT PAVING of all kinds.

Gold (W fr 138 S 2d) & fr Gray's Ferry av) now Moravian
Gold (C Hill) now Sprague
Good (Gtn) now Sharpnack
Goodwater now St James
Goodwill al now N Watts
Goodwin now Ludlow
Goodwin (S fr St James, W of S 7th) now S Perth
Gothic now Sansom
Grace now Appletree
Graff now Winter
Grafton ct now Beck
Graham now Seybert
Grand (W P) now Fitzwater
Grant (W fr S 9th, S of Moore) now Sigel
Grant (Gtn) now Shirley
Grant av now Clifford
Granville now Cypress
Gray (115 Poplar) now Hope
Gray (Richmond to E Allen) now Day
Gray's la (N fr Market to Haverford) now Redfield
Graydon now N Mole
Grayson now Folsom
Green (Fkd) now Womrath
Green (N Town) now Roy
Green (W P) W fr N 40th to N Preston now Brandywine
Green la now E Kerbaugh
Green's ct now Quarry
Green Hill now N Smedley
Grindstone al now N Philip
Griscom now S Lawrence
Griswold's al now S Randolph
Grove now Edwin
Grover now S Howard
Grover's la (P'ville) now Welcome
Grubb now Latimer
Guilford now S American
Guirey (Dickinson to Passy'k av) now Greenwich
Guirey (Dickinson to S 12th) now Wilder
Gulielma now Naudain
Gunner now Hurley
Haas now N Croskey
Hackley now Hewson
Hagert (Ktn av to Aramingo av) now Adams
Hagert (N 13th to N Clarion) now Letterly
Hagey (W P) (W fr N 73d, N of Columbia av) now Sherwood
Hagy's Mill rd (Roxb) now Hagy
Haines (946 S 12th) now Harper
Hall now N Orianna

Hall (W P) now Appletree
Hallowell now Kimball
Hamilton (Myk) now Wilde
Hamilton (Tac) now Rawle
Hammond now Harper
Hampton now Addison
Hancock (McKean, W of S 2d) now S Philip
Hancock (Gtn) now Baynton
Hand now Waverly
Hanley now S Fairhill
Hannah now Herman
Hanover now E Columbia av
Hanson (W P) (S 49th to Hanson) now Reinhard
Hare now Aspen
Harker (Gtn) now Physic
Harman av now S Beechwood
Harmony (770 S 4th) now Fulton
Harmony ct (404 S 6th) now Waverly
Harmstead now Rodman
Harper (Fkd) now Romain
Harriet now Salmon
Harrison (1737 Howard) now Palmer
Harrison (Myk) now St David's
Harrison av now N Dover
Harrowgate la now E Atlantic
Harshaw now S Opal
Hart now Euclid
Harvard now N Beechwood
Harvey now S Rosewood
Harvey pl (Gtn) now Concord
Hatton pl now N Mildred
Haviland pl now Winter
Hawthorne (W P) now Trinity
Haydock now Pollard
Hays now Earp
Hazel now Pierce
Hazel av (1419 Clearfield) now N Rosewood
Hazelwood now S Bonsall
Hazzard (Ktn av to Coral) now E Hazzard
Heath now Cambridge
Heberton now Chancellor
Hedding now N Sydenham
Heins now Panama
Helmuth now Waverly
Henderson av now Hazzard
Henrietta now Seybert
Henry (W fr Howard, N of Ontario) now Estaugh
Henry (S fr Waverly, W of S 11th) now S Jessup
Henry (Gtn) now Keyser
Henry (Tac) now Lucas
Hepburn now S Smedley

RICHARDSON & ROSS, 30th & Race Sts.

HER CHANGES IN NAMES OF STREETS. JUN 11

Herbine av now Morse
Herman (N 26th to 32d) now Gordon
Hermitage now Galloway
Hewitt pl now De Lancey
Hewson now E Seltzer
Heyer pl now St James
Hibberd now N Sartain
Hickey now S Mole
Hides' ct now Cuthbert
Hides ct (E & W) now N Schell
Higgins ct now S Howard
Hill now Clymer
Hill (Myk) now Dexter
Hill now Dillman
Hillary now S Garnet
Hillsdale now N Orianna
Hillside av (Roxb) now Burnside
Hoadley (W P) now Hanson
Hobensack av (C Hill) now Para
Hockley now Miller
Hoffman (W P) now Noble
Holland pl (E & W) now Myrtle
Holland pl (N & S)now N Warnock
Hollinger now N Patton
Holly now S Mole
Holman now Martha
Holmes now Wood
Home pl now S Reese
Honeysuckle av (Hbg) now Ditman
Hopkins (W P) now Alden
Horstmann now N Van Pelt
Howard (fr 2217 Aspen) now N Croskey
Howard (Myk) now 11 Burnside
Howard (N Town) now Ruffner
Howell (S 19th to S 20th) now De Lancey
Howell (Bdg) now Edgemont
Howell (Fkd) now Pratt
Howell (W P) now Cherry
Hubbell now S Mildred
Hubbs now Redner
Hudson (S fr 316 Market) now S Orianna
Hudson (W fr Miller) now E Sterner
Hull now E Elkhart
Humboldt (E fr N 11th to P & R Rw) now E Russell
Humboldt (W fr N 22d to N 23d) now Firth
Hummel now Annin
Hunter (19 N 10th) now Commerce
Hunter (Bdg) now Berkshire
Hunter's Row now Cypress
Hunt's la now E Seltzer
Hurst now S Randolph
Illinois now S Bouvier
Ingersoll (N 18th to N 19th) now Kershaw

Inglis now Ionic
Innes now Sarah
Ireland now Memphis
Irvin now Brandywine
Irving (Bdg) now Haworth
Irving (W P) (W fr N 48th) now Wallace
Isabella (S E fr Coral) now E Silver
Itschner now Hilton
Ivy now Naudain
Jackson (E fr 2655 Trenton av) now Oakdale
Jackson (S fr 1022 Wash'n av) now S Alder
Jackson (W fr N 8th to N 9th) now Schiller
Jackson (Bln) now Gregg
Jackson (Myk) (Wright to Umbria) now Canton
Jackson (Myk) (Baker to Main) now Carson
Jacob now Lardner
Jacoby now N Camac
James now E Mayfield
James (Falls) now Stanton
Jamison now Manton
Jane now Kauffman
Jarden now S Capitol
Jarvis (S 3d to S 4th) now Gerritt
Jarvis (Moyam'g av to Dickinson) now Wilder
Java pl now N Hutchinson
Jay now N Darien
Jayne now Ranstead
Jefferson (S 17th, S of Walnut) now Latimer
Jefferson (Fkd) now Ditman
Jefferson (Myk) now Wright
Jefferson (Roxb) now Hermitage
Jefferson (W P) (Belmont av to Leidy) now Thompson
Jenkins now Filbert
Jennett av (Myk) now Rochelle av
John (W fr Mascher) now Atlantic
John (Bdg) now Miller
John (Myk) now Dexter
Johnson (Fkd) now Elizabeth
Johnston (W fr 18 S 19th) now Ranstead
Jones (14 N 17th) now Commerce
Jones (N fr Rodman) now S Fairhill
Jones (W P) now Quarry
Judge now E Toronto
Julia now N Hancock
Julianna now N Randolph
June (756 S 7th) now St Albans
Juniata (416 Gerritt) now S Lawrence

ASPHALTUM BLOCKS and TILES.

SHRIVER, BARTLETT & CO. {ADJUSTMENTS COLLECTIONS

Juvenal now S Clifton
Kansas now Catharine
Kates (1511 Federal) now S Hicks
Kates (S Mole to S Rosewood) now Webster
Kay now Hagert
Keble row Addison
Keefe now Titan
Keeler's la now Hoffman
Keeley's al (Myk) now St Davids
Keffer (W P) now Natrona
Kelton now N Carlisle
Kemble now Waverly
Kempton now Manning
Kenderton now N Watts
Kennedy now Culvert
Kent now Panama
Kenyon now N Bodine
Kerr (S fr 2218 Pine) now S Croskey
Kerr (W fr N Lawrence) now Myrtle
Kershaw (N fr 1441 Cherry) now Burns
Kessler now N Percy
Kettlewell now E Schiller
Keyser (1019 E Columbia av) now E Wilt
Kildare now Ralston
Kingston (W fr 202 S 13th) now Chancellor
Kimmler (Gtn) now Lena
Klauder now Morse
Kline (W P) now Chancellor
Kneass now Waverly
Knight's ct (S fr 912 Cherry) now Appletree
Knight's ct now N Schell
Knorr (2513 A) now Potter
Knox (921 Brown) now N Hutchinson
Kressler now N Randolph
Krider al now Pemberton
Kulp now Alsop
Kurtz now N Jessup
Kyser now Emory
Lafayette (1156 S 9th) now Annin
Lafayette (Gtn) now Haines
Lagrange (W fr 40 N 2d) now Filbert
Lagrange (S fr 1338 Carpenter) now S Watts
Lambert (fr E Clearfield) now E Allen
Lambert (224 N 13th) now Florist
Lambrecht now Cornwall
Lancaster now S Howard
Lancaster (W P) (Market to 33d) now Ludlow

Landis now Manning
Landreth now Quarry
Larch now N Alder
Lardner now Manning
Lark now Weikel
Larkin now S Swanson
Latch av (Myk) now Mansion
Latimer (E Susq'ana av) now Harper
Laurel (Gtn) now Woodlawn
Lava pl now St James
Lavinia now Rodman
Lawnton now N Warnock
Lawrence av now Earp
Lawson now N Marvine
Lebanon now S Hutchinson
Leaf (Catharine W of S 7th) now S Perth
Leaf (W P) (S 32d to S 33d) now Moravian
Leamy now B
Ledger pl (E & W) now Cuthbert
Ledger pl (N & S) now N American
Lee (28 S 18th) now Ranstead
Lee av (W P) now Kershaw
Leeds av now N Carlisle
Lehman (Gtn) now Price
Leib now Blair
Leibert (Myk) now Silverwood
Leiper (19 S 13th) now Ludlow
Leiper (Ludlow to Ranstead) now S Camac
Lena (N 17th N of Cayuga) now Blavis
Lentz now Latona
Leon now S Clifton
Letitia (S fr Snyder av) now S Hancock
Levant now S American
Leverine av (Gtn) now Nippon
Lewis (W P) now Moravian
Lex (fr N 15th) now Harmer
Liberty (W P) now Sloan
Library now Sansom
Lily Ann now S Clifton
Lincoln av (P'ville) now Glenmore
Linda now Monmouth
Linden (923 Spg Garden) now N Percy
Linden (Fkd) now Herbert
Linden (Myk) (Fountain to Ripka) now Sheldon
Linden (Myk) (Ripka to Greenough) now Fowler
Linden sq now Colona
Lindsay now S Bancroft
Lindsay's av now S Marvine
Lingo now S Bouvier

RICHARDSON & ROSS, 30th & Race Sts.

CLAIMS AND LITIGATED MATTERS.

Linn now Noble
Linnard now Sears
Linney now E Atlantic
Linton pl now Ionic
Linville now Taylor
Linwood (W P) now Folsom
Lisbon (Lippincott to Clearfield) now N Chadwick
Lisbon (S 6th to S Reese) now Rodman
Lisle now S Mildred
Lissner now E Walter
Little Belt pl now Salter
Little Foulkrod (Fkd) now Glenlock
Little Mechlin (Gtn) now Clapier
Little Medina now Medina
Little Wayne (Gtn) now Keyser
Lloyd (N fr 2057 Sergeant) now Kern
Lloyd (S fr Kater) now S Rosewood
Lloyd (P'ville) now Yocum
Locust (S 6th to S Franklin) now Irving
Locust (S 18th to S 19th) now Rittenhouse sq
Locust (Bdg) now Kennedy
Locust av (Gtn) now Maplewood
Lodge (S American to S 2d) now Sansom
Lodge (Ludlow to Ranstead) now S Perth
Logan (N 20th & Butler) now Blaine
Logan av (N 13th ab Somerset) now Rush
Long now S Hutchinson
Lorain now Perth
Louisa av now S Howard
Loyal now E Cabot
Lucy now E Dakota
Lukens now Alter
Lybrand now N Watts
Lydia (C Hill) now Benczet
Lydia (W P) now June
Lynch now Marion
Lynd now Wallace
Lyndall al now Chancellor
McAllister al now Quarry
McClellan (1217 E Montg'y av) now E Walter
McClellan (816 Pennock) now Reno
McCormick av now Quarry
McCrea now Fulton
McCurdy now Alter
McFall now Pennock
McFarland (W P) now Ollve
McGrath now N Leithgow
McIlravey (S Sartain to S Jessup) now Hall

McIlravey (Montrose to Hall) now S Jessup
McIlravey (N & S) now S Sartain
McIlwain now Titan
McKean's ct now S Wendle
McMullen's ct now S Leithgow
McMurray now Webb
McNally now Judson
McNeile av now S Watts
Mackinaw now Summer
Madison (N fr 1117 Race) now N Marvine
Madison (W fr N 24th) now Carlton
Madison (P'ville) now Barrett
Madison (Tac) now Barton
Magnet (Myk) now Fleming
Magnolia now N Randolph
Main (Myk) (N W fr Leverington) now Nixon
Malvern now Helen
Manakin now N Reese
Manilla now Montrose
Manley (W P) now Sharswood
Manor row Cadwallader
Manship now S Sartain
Mansion (629 York) now N Sheridan
Maple (W fr N 8th, N of Race) now Spring
Maple (Norris E of N Front) now Trenton av
Maple av now N Mole
Maple av (Olney) now Ella
Marble now Ludlow
Marble ct now S Watts
Margaretta (S fr League) now S Sheridan
Margaretta (W fr 418 N Front) now Produce av
Maria now Olive
Marion now Manton
Marker now Mountain
Markham now Swain
Markle (Myk & Roxb) (Markle to Seville) now Dexter
Markle (Myk) (Leukon to Myk av) now Seville
Mark's la now Quarry
Marriott now Montrose
Marshall (Gtn) now Schuyler
Marston (Quarry to Appletree) now N Clarion
Marston (W P) now Lombard
Martin now S Garnet
Martin's ct (206 Carpenter) now S American
Marvine (Stiles W of N 11th) now N Sartain
Mary (1219 S 7th) now Manton

SHEET ASPHALT PAVING of all kinds.

SHRIVER, BARTLETT & CO. {ADJUSTMENTS COLLECTIONS}

Mary (W fr 962 S Front) now League
Mary (Tac) now Knorr
Mast now N Reese
Mather now N Sydenham
Matlack (E fr 1611 Howard) now Guest
Matlack (N fr 1925 Parrish) now N Opal
May (750 S 7th) now Clymer
May (Gtn) now Mayland
Mayfield (N 6th to N 7th) now Commissioner
Mayland now N Randolph
Maynard pl now S Howard
Mead now Fitzwater
Meadow (W P) now S Markoe
Mechanic (506 Carpenter) now League
Mechanic (Carpenter to League) now S Reese
Mechanic (Myk) now Roxborough
Mechlin (Gtn) (Gtn av to Wakefield) now Clapier
Mechlin (Gtn) (fr Baynton S W) now E Clapier
Medical now Moravian
Medina (1312 S 7th) now Sears
Meehan now S Jessup
Mehl (Gtn) now E Seymour
Meighan now E Lippincott
Melcher now N Randolph
Melloy now Ranstead
Melrose (W P) now Pearl
Mendenhall now S Bouvier
Mendon pl now Hamilton
Mercer (Gtn) now Rubicam
Merchant now Ludlow
Mercury now E Cabot
Meredith (N 23d to N 24th) now Perot
Meredith (Fbg) now Hess
Merion av (W P) now Stewart
Merion rd (W P) now N 65th
Mervine (See N & S Marvine)
Metcalf now Kenilworth
Middle al now Panama
Middleton now Dreer
Midvale (N Town) now Blabon
Miles al now Chancellor
Mill (Fkd) now Vandike
Mill (Gtn) (N 20th to Gtn av) now Church la
Mill (Gtn) (N 20th to Old York rd) now Spencer
Miller (803 Wash'n av) now S Darien
Miller (Gtn) (Wister to Shedaker) now Sheldon

Miller (Gtn) (Gtn av to Cresheim) now E Durham
Miller (W P) now Sloan
Millman now Hall
Milton now Montrose
Minerva now Brandywine
Minnesota (W P) now Irving
Minor now Ludlow
Minster now Addison
Mint ct now Quarry
Mintzer now Galloway
Mohawk av (Gtn) now Mechanic
Monastery av (Myk) now Levering
Monitor pl now N Wendle
Monroe (2631 Poplar) now Chang
Monroe (Myk) now Linney
Monroe (Tac) now Princeton
Monroe av (W P) now Thompson
Montana (Gray's Ferry av to Reed) now S Shedwick
Montcalm now S Percy
Monterey now Summer
Monument av now Hewson
Moore (E fr Emerald) now E Fletcher
Moore (746 S Juniper) now Clymer
Morgan (Wood to Vine) now N Bodine
Morgan (N 9th to N 11th) now Winter
Moro now S Fawn
Morrell (H'ville) now Harlan
Morris (Helen, N of E Lehigh av) now E Seltzer
Morton now Burleigh
Norton av now S Orianna
Mosley now Wilder
Moss now Aunin
Mount Holly now S Colorado
Mount Pleasant now Cabot
Mount Vernon (Myk) now Gates
Mount Vernon (W P) (N 41st to Preston) now Olive
Moyer now Eminence
Moyer's al (Myk) now Ring
Mulberry (Myk) now Carson
Mulberry al now Summer
Mulberry av (W P) now Waverly
Mulford (S Randolph to S Reese) now Alter
Mulford (Alter to Ellsworth) S Reese
Mullen now Tilton
Muller now S Stillman
Mulloney now St James
Mundell now Seltzer
Murray's av now Monterey
Mustin ct now Summer

RICHARDSON & ROSS, 30th & Race Sts.

Myrtle (N fr E Clearfield, E of Bath) now Balfour
Nash (Gtn) (Phil-Ellena to Sharpnack) now Ross
Nash (Gtn) (Walnut la to Haines) now Magnolia
Nassau (150 N 9th) now Quarry
Native now Hall
Natrona (Diamond, W of N 3d) now Douglas
Naylor now Latona
Neff (Myk) now Evergreen
Nelson pl now Westmont
Nelson's ct now Senate
Neville pl now N Fairhill
New (C Hill) now Newton
New (Fkd) now Fillmore
New Rowland (Hbg) now Fairview
Newbold (Ruscomb to Rockland) now N Uber
Newbold (Pearl to Shamokin) now N Uber
Newcomb (N Town) now Lowe
Newkirk (2669 E Cumberland) now Webb
Newkumet (N fr Vine) now N 24th
Newkumet (N 24th to N Bonsall) now Winter
Newton now S Leithgow
Nice av (Blue Bell Hill) now Johnson
Nicholas now S Spangler
Nicholson now N Sheridan
Norris (Gtn) now Norman
North (34 N 5th) now Cuthbert
North (P'ville) now Saybrook
N Albion (Cherry to Vine) now N Van Pelt
N Albion (Arch to Cherry) now N Beechwood
N Broad (fr P & T R R, E of Haworth) now Pratt
N East av now Cabot
N 5½ now N Reese
N 15th (fr Indiana N) now N Hicks
N 15½ now N Sydenham
N 17¼ now N Colorado
N 17½ now N Bouvier
N 19¼ now N Garnet
N 19½ now N Uber
N 19¾ now N Opal
N 25½ now N Stillman
N 25¾ now N Rambrey
N 27½ now Marston
N 29½ now Hollywood
N 30½ now Corlies
N 30¾ now Stanley
N 31½ now N Napa
N 31¾ now N Patton

N 32½ now Natrona
N 32¾ now Douglas
N 33½ (Falls) now Osmond
N 33½ now N Spangler
N 36½ (W P) now N McAlpin
N 39¼ (W P) now State
N 39½ (W P) now Union
N 39¾ (W P) now Sloan
N 42¾ (W P) now Hutton
N 43½ (W P) now Pallas
N 44½ (W P) now Mica
N 46¾ (W P) now N May
N 47½ (W P) now Moss
N 48½ (W P) now N Fallon
N 49½ (W P) now St Bernard
N 50½ (W P) now N Farson
N 51½ (W P) now Paxon
N 52½ (W P) now Wilton
N 53½ (W P) now Peach
N 54½ (W P) now N Conestoga
N 54¾ (W P) now Sickels
N 55½ (W P) now N Allison
N 57½ (W P) now Alden
N 58½ (W P) now Wanamaker
N 59½ (W P) now Redfield
N 60½ (W P) now N Edgewood
N 61½ (W P) now Robinson
N 62½ (W P) now N Felton
N 63½ (W P) now Gross
N 64½ (W P) now Simpson
N 65½ (W P) now Daggett
N 66½ (P'ville) now Shields
N 72½ (W P) now Anna
Norton (Gtn) now Cliveden
Norwood (Gtn) now Isabella
Norwood av now N Garnet
Norwood av (C Hill) now Sullivan
Oak (Myk) now Conarroe
Oak (W P) now Melville
Oakford pl now S Bodine
Ocean now Hope
Ohio now Waverly
Old Meadow (Fkd) now Wilmot
Oliver (Lewis to Luzerne) now Emery
Oliver (W fr 916 S 10th) now Salter
Olivia pl now E Pacific
Olney (Gtn) now Abbotsford
Onas now Olive
Ontario (N fr 1335 Parrish) now N Watts
Onyx (Bdg) now Melvale
Orange (C Hill) now Para
Orchard (N & S fr Reno) now N Orkney
Orchard (Bdg) now Salmon
Orion (W P) now N Shedwick
Osage av (W P) now Waverly

ASPHALTUM BLOCKS and TILES.

Osborne's ct now Chancellor
Oscar now S Stanley
Osprey now Ringgold
Otsego (N fr E Somerset) now N Swanson
Otsego (S fr 23 Christian) now S Water
Otter (999 N 2d) now Wildey
Otto (Gtn) now N Norwood
Outlet now Clay
Overbrook (Tac) now Gillespie
Ovington now S Schell
Owen (1412 S 5th) now Gerritt
Owen (Bucknell to Judson) now Nectarine
Owen (W of N 22d) now N Bucknell
Pagoda now Taylor
Pallas (Tasker to Porter, W of S 12th) now S Camac
Palm (913 Olive) now N Hutchinson
Palo Alto row S Capitol
Panama now Latimer
Parade now Titan
Paradise al now N Leithgow
Parham now Clymer
Park (1820 Fitzwater) now Dorrance
Park (1206 S 27th) now Manton
Park (N 17th, N of Clearfield) now Wishart
Park (N 20th, N of Clearfield) now Lippincott
Park ter (N 27th, N of Fairmount av) now Folsom
Park ter (N Taney to N 26th) now Swain
Parker now S Randolph
Pascal now Kimball
Paschall av (W P) now Linmore
Path now N Hicks
Patton (Gtn) now Priscilla
Paul (1028 S 6th) now League
Paxton now Ellsworth
Peach (153 Green) now N Hancock
Peach (Fkd) now Cloud
Pear (W fr S 2d) now Chancellor
Pear (W P) now N Harmony
Peltz (Myk) now Siddall
Pemberton (Mt. Vernon to Wallace) now N Watts
Pemberton (N fr Sansom, W of S 2d) now S Philip
Pembroke (N of Butler to Erie av) now N Watts
Pembroke pl now Florist
Penn (4 Pine) now S Water
Penn (Bdg) now Mercer

Penn (Myk) (Ridge av to Terrace) now Pensdale
Penn (Myk) (Umbria to P & R R W) now Gates
Penn (Tac) now Knorr
Penn al (Carlton to Callowhill) now N Bodine
Penn al (W fr 336 N American) now Carlton
Pennington now S Bodine
Pennock (W P) now Lansdowne av
Pennsylvania av (N fr Summer) now N Randolph
Pepper now Albert
Perkins now Salter
Perot (N 25th to N 26th) now Olive
Perry now N Clarion
Peters (W of S 11th, S of Ellsworth) now S Jessup
Peters' al now Reno
Petroleum now S Hancock
Pharo now Cleveland
Philadelphia now N Sydenham
Pike now N Iseminger
Pinder (Gtn) now Earlham
Pink now N Orianna
Placid pl now Beck
Plane now Sears
Pleffenberg pl now N Schell
Plover now Ellsworth
Ployd (Gtn) now Mechanic
Plume pl now Addison
Pomeroy av now Boston
Poplar (Myk) now St Davids
Porcelain now Moravian
Portland now Shamokin
Powell now De Lancey
Prescott (W P) now Olive
Preston (Wallace, W of N 0th) now N Hutchinson
Prime now Ellsworth
Pritchett now Annin
Proctor sq (W P) now Chancellor
Prospect now N Delhi
Prospect (Roxb) now Lemonte
Prune (Fkd) now Pear
Pryor's ct now Manning
Pullinger (W P) now Natrona
Putnam now Turner
Quarry ct now N Stillman
Quince now S Marvine
Race (Hbg) now Holmesburg
Rachel now N Hancock
Raggio now S Lawrence
Rainbow now Dreer
Ralston now Addison
Raspberry al now S Hutchinson
Ratcliffe now S Perth

RICHARDSON & ROSS, 30th & Race Sts.

Rawle (N 5th, N of Brown) now Reno
Rawle (Reed, W of S 8th) now S Darien
Reckless now League
Redwood now Manton
Reilly (W P) now Peach
Relief now Naudain
Rementer al now Cuthbert
Rentschler now N Marvine
Renwick (W P) now S Allison
Rex av (Gtn & C Hill) now Summit av
Rhoades now Shamokin
Richard now Addison
Richardson now S Mole
Richfield (W fr N 9th, N of Somerset) now Auburn
Richfield (N Marshall to N 7th & fr N 12th to Glenwood av) now Rush
Ridge (Fkd) now Gillingham
Ridgeway ter now N Taney
Ridley av now Miller
Riggs now Webster
Rihl now Sepviva
Riley (Myk) now Dupont
Ringgold now Kimball
Ringgold pl now Waverly
Ristine (N fr Spring) now N Mildred
Ristine (S14 Jackson) now S Mildred
Ritchie now S Watts
Rittenhouse now Rittenhouse sq
Robbins (Kenilworth to Pemberton) now S Darien
Robert (Myk) now Aurania
Roberts now Hope
Robeson (Myk) now Rector
Robinson now Salmon
Rochford now Ralston
Rockland (W P) now Brandywine
Rodgers al now N Howard
Rodman (Falls) now Roscoe
Rodney now Panama
Ronaldson now S Delhi
Rorer (C Hill) (N 17th, N of 72d av, N) now Plymouth
Rorer (C Hill) (Hartwell to Arlington) now Shawnee
Rose (Almond to Moyer) now E Letterly
Rose (W fr 710 S 13th) now Kenilworth
Rose al (1009 Locust) now S Alder
Rose al (W P) now S McAlpin
Rosemont now Clementine
Rosette (Gtn) now Wister
Ross (Wildey to Richmond) now Earl
Ross (Gtn) now Magnolia

Roth (Sepviva to Memphis) now Earl
Rowland's ct now N Perth
Royal (Gtn) now Portico
Rugan now N Hutchinson
Rule (W fr S Hancock, S of Wharton) now Earp
Rule (S 4th, S of Reed) now Gerritt
Rundle now De Lancey
Rural av (Gtn) now Mower
Rush (N Broad, N of Indiana) now Toronto
Russell (S fr 832 Bainbridge) now S Schell
Russell (W fr 1012 S 3d) now Kimball
Russell (Gtn) now Slocum
Rye (Quarry to Cherry) now N Alder
Rye (Manton to Gerritt) now S Philip
Sacramento av now Emery
St Alban's now Clymer
St Ann av now Agate
St David now N Bonsall
St John now N American
St Joseph's av now Ranstead
St Mark's sq (N Town) now Lowe
St Paul's av now Fulton
Salem al now Addison
Sanderson now Manton
Sarah (Wiss) now Bridget
Saranac now Gerritt
Saulnier now Walter
Savannah now E Allen
Savery now E Oxford
Saxon now E Wisbart
Schaffer (Gtn) now Morton
Schneider av now Arlington
Schollenberger av now Arcadia
School (Bdg) now Mercer
Scipio pl now Cuthbert
Scott (908 N 19th) now George
Scott (1432 S 8th) now Wilder
Seibold now S Colorado
Selfridge now S Colorado
Selig (Myk) now Lawnton
Seminole (Gtn) now Underhill
Senate now Monroe
Seneca (W P) now Parrish
Seniff now Ionic
Sergeant (222 N 9th) now Spring
Sewell now Janney
Sewer (W P) now Lowber
Seybert (N 18th N of Thompson) now Ingersoll
Shamokin (N Front to N 2d) now Produce av
Shaw's la (Roxb) now Isabella
Sheaff now Spring

2

SHEET ASPHALT PAVING of all kinds.

Shellbark now Quarry
Sherborne pl (W P) now Regent
Shields now S Hancock
Shoch (2025 Market) now N Capitol
Shock (N fr Fitzwater, E of S Front) now S Water
Shoemaker now Ludlow
Shoemaker (Gtn) now Rubicam
Shoemaker's ct new Kenyon
Short (Tac) now James
Showaker now Oakdale
Shur's la (Myk & Roxb) now Walnut la
Sidmouth now S Franklin
Sidney now S Darien
Silbert now S Warnock
Silliman (W P) now Hutton
Siloam now Livingston
Silver (22 N 12th) now Commerce
Silver (W P) now Hoopes
Simes now Ludlow
Simmons now Myrtlewood
Sisty now N Delhi
Slossman now Laurel
Smedley (W P) now Pearl
Smith now Lippincott
Smith's ct (529 Lombard) now S Fairhill
Sober now S Capitol
Somerville (Gtn av to N 12th) now Silver
Somerville (N 26th to N 27th) now Sterner
Senora now N Alder
Sorrel now E Monmouth
Souder now Waverly
S Albion now S Van Pelt
S Juniper (Wharton to Titan) now S Watts
S Marshall (1122 S 13th) now Alter
S Pearl (Locust, W of S 11th) now S Jessup
S Pearl (S Jessup, S of Locust) now Latimer
S Watts (S 20th to S Uber) now Waverly
S 7th (Walnut to Irving) now S Franklin
S 40¼ (W P) now S Preston
S 41½ (W P) now S Holly
S 45¼ (W P) now S Melville
S 46½ (W P) now S Markoe
S 46¾ (W P) now S May
S 48¼ (W P) now S Fallon
S 50½ (W P) now S Farson
S 54½ (W P) now S Conestoga
S 55½ (W P) now S Allison
S 56½ (W P) now S Frazier
S 60½ (W P) now S Edgewood

S 62½ (W P) now S Felton
S 66½ (W P) now Shields
Spafford now S Marshall
Spangler (N fr Moyer) now Ritter
Sparks (Bdg) now Tilton
Spencer (Falls) now Calumet
Spencer ter (W P) now Winter
Spring (2553 E Somerset) now Livingston
Spring (Commissioner to Ann) now Miller
Spring (N 22d to N Van Pelt) now Summer
Spring (N 20th to N Opal) now Winter
Spring (Fkd) now Cloud
Spring (Myk) now Carson
Spring (Roxb) now Streeper
Spring (Tac) now Mason
Spring (W P) now Reinhard
Spring al (Myk) now Carson
Springett now North
Square now Sears
Stanley now Pemberton
Stapleton now S Bodine
Starr now S Darien
Starr al now N Fairhill
Steadman now Manning
Steam Mill al now Pegg
Steinmetz pl (W P) now S Shedwick
Stella (21st wd) now Cunard
Stephen (1248 N 26th) now Stiles
Stephen (N fr Water) now Etting
Stirling now S Chadwick
Stetson av now N Leithgow
Stewart (fr Fitzwater) now S Delhi
Stewart (1410 N 21st) now Harlan
Stewart (E fr S 21st, S of Walnut) now Latimer
Stewart (W Moyam'g av, W of S 9th) now S Hutchinson
Stocker now S Colorado
Stockton now S Iseminger
Stoeckel now N Lambert
Stone now Waverly
Stratford pl now St James
Strawbridge now Archer
Stretch now S Norwood
Struthers now Winter
Suffolk now League
Sugden now Lippincott
Sumac now Hazzard
Summer (Lehigh av to Auburn & fr Orthodox S, N E of E Thompson) now Mercer
Summer (N 21st to N 22d) now Spring
Suplee (W P) now Poplar

RICHARDSON & ROSS, 30th & Race Sts.

CLAIMS AND LITIGATED MATTERS.

Susanna now E Boston
Sussex now N Sartain
Sutherland now S Hancock
Sutherland av now Schuylkill av
Swarthmore pl now Summer
Sycamore (Locust to Spruce) now S Watts
Sycamore (Olney) now Kip
Sycamore (Cheltenham av to Plymouth) now N Smedley
Sydney now S Darien
Sylvan (W P) now Wyalusing
Sylvan av (Hbg) now Cottage
Sylvester now Mountain
Tabassa (N 9th to N 10th) now Boston
Talbot pl (W P) now De Lancey
Talmage now N Philip
Tamarind now Hope
Tan la (Fkd) now Cloud
Tanner now S Leithgow
Tappen pl now N Beulah
Tatlow now Noble
Taylor (2421 Ktn av) now E Boston
Taylor (3906 N Broad) now Bott
Taylor (W fr S Marshall) now Greenwich
Taylor (Bdg) now Brill
Taylor (Fkd) now Brill
Temperance pl now Pemberton
Temple now Kimball
Tenor pl now Addison
Thames now E Seltzer
Thayer now Harlan
Thomas (Fkd) (N fr Longshore) now Eadom
Thomas (Fkd) (N fr 15 Tacony) now Salem
Thomas (Roxb) now Manatawna
Thomas av (1605 York) now N Bancroft
Thomazine now Turner
Thompson (Myk) now Mansion
Thouron now N Fairhill
Thurlow now Webster
Tiernan now S Carlisle
Timothy now N Jessup
Tisdale pl now S Bodine
Tivoli now Stella
Toland now Quarry
Toledo (W P) now Stiles
Ton al now Gatzmer
Torpin now Melvale
Torr (Ridge av to N 9th) now Carlton
Torr (W P) now Thompson
Tower now Appletree
Townsend now E Fletcher

Trellis (S Front, S of Tasker) now Mountain
Trellis (fr Mountain, W of S Front) now S Hancock
Tremont pl (W P) now Budd
Trinity pl now Cypress
Trotter now S Lee
Troubat av (Oak la) now N 9th
Trout now Katel
Truxton now S Fawn
Tudor now S Franklin
Turner (Allegheny av to Butler) now N Randolph
Tyler now Hall
Tyson now Cadwallader
Ulrich now N Orkney
Union (W fr 326 S Front) now De Lancey
Union (Tac) now National
Union (W P) (Aspen to Brown, W of N 36th) now N McAlpin
Union av (Oak la) now N 7th
Upland Way (W P) now N 60th
Urbanna pl now N Percy
Valeria now Parrish
Vandalia (C Hill) now Shawnee
Vandeveer now S Delhi
Vanhorn (Hbg) now Craig
Vanilla (W P) now Pearl
Vasey now Panama
Vaughn now S Sydenham
Vermont pl now Cambridge
Verner now S Taney
Vernon now Reno
Victoria now S Iseminger
Vincent now N Philip
Virginia (S E fr 3163 Amber) now E Wishart
Virginia (W fr 706 N 22d) now Olive
Vista now S Opal
Volkmar now E Walter
Vollum now Fawn
Wabash (Myk) now Smick
Wager now Cambridge
Wagner now S Sartain
Waldron now Harper
Walker (William to Aramingo av) now Miller
Walker av (B Town) now N Opal
Wall now Webster
Waln now S Beulah
Walnut (Myk) now Mallory
Walnut pl (W P) now S Harmony
Ward now Cleveland
Warder now Blair
Warner (Myk) now Kingsley
Warren (W P) (W fr N 38th, N of Powelton av) now Pearl
Warthman's ct now E Dakota

ASPHALTUM BLOCKS and TILES.

Washington (W fr N 27th) now Kershaw
Washington (Fkd) (Glenloch to James) now Haworth
Washington (Myk) now Umbria
Washington (Tac & Hbg) now Disston
Washington av (Fkd) (Meadow to S W of Orthodox) now Hawthorne
Water (Fkd) now Milnor
Waterloo (Allegheny av N of Tioga) now Collins
Waterloo (Mascher, N of Berks) now Hewson
Watt (fr S Uber) now Waverly
Wayne (923 Mt Vernon) now N Hutchinson
Wayne (W fr Tulip) now E William
Wayne Ter (Gtn) now Dennie
Weaver (519 Green) now N Randolph
Weaver (Gtn) now Mayland
Webb now S Chadwick
Webster (Myk) now Fleming
Weccacoe now S Leithgow
Weiss (Gtn) now N Beechwood
Weisser (Bdg) now Fillmore
Wellington (Ktn av to Aramingo av) now E Madison
Wellington (South to Bainbridge) now S 26th
Wentz (Olney) now N Water
West now N Uber
W College av now N Stillman
W Walnut la (Myk) now Walnut la
W Washington av (Myk) now Wash'n la
W Washington sq (S 7th) now S Franklin
Wetherill now S Carlisle
Wharton la now Greenwich
Wheat (1325 Fkd av) now Mercer
Wheat (130 Manton) now S Hancock
Wheat (Quarry to Cherry) now N Clifton
Wheat (E & W fr N Alder) now Quarry
Whelan now Atlantic
Whitby av now Birch
White (709 S 15th) now Kenilworth
Whitecars row now Manning
Whitehall now Nectarine
Whitney (1010 Passyunk av) now Kimball
Whittler (Gtn) now Newhall
Wilcox (W fr 328 S 19th) now Panama

Willard now Hilton
William (Drexel to Walker) now Bright
Williams (E fr 251 S 21st) now Latimer
Williams (Myk) now Dearnley
Williamson now Pierce
Willig av now Livingston
Willington (Susq'ana av to Lehigh av) now N Chadwick
Willow av (Gtn) now Morton
Wilmer now Carlton
Wilson (952 S Water) now Kimball
Wilson (S 20th to S 21st) now Clymer
Wilson (Norris to Fletcher & York to Dauphin) now Mercer
Wilson (Milestown) now N Bancroft
Winchester (Myk) now St Davids
Windrim now Weymouth
Windsor sq now Woodstock
Winfried pl now Appletree
Wingohocking (Gtn) now Nash
Winslow now Spring
Wistar now Brandywine
Wistar's al now Filbert
Wisteria av (Gtn) now Shedaker
Wood (Fkd) now Frogmoor
Wood (Myk) now Silverwood
Woodbine (612 Federal) now S Marshall
Woodbine av (Gtn) now Woodlawn
Woodland (W P) now De Lancey
Woodward (W P) now St Mark's
Worth now Cross
Wrekin now E Harold
Wright (N 21st, S of Jefferson) now Stewart
Wright (221 Ontario) now Dillman
Wyalusing av (Gtn) now Luray
Wyatt now Alter
Wykoff (W P) now Peach
Wynkoop now Irving
Wynn (Gtn) now Duncannon
Wyoming (N E fr Ann) now Martha
Wyoming (1504 Bainbridge) now S Hicks
Wyoming (1320 S 2d) now Earp
Wyoming (W P) now N Preston
Y P M pl now S Orianna
Yardley now N Lambert
Yhost now S Reese
Young (612 Wolf) now S Marshall
Young (Bdg) now Almond
Zenobia now St James

RICHARDSON & ROSS, 30th & Race Sts.

KEY TO STREET NAMES.

NORTH AND SOUTH STREETS, WEST OF NORTH AND SOUTH FRONT.

Front
Hope
Howard
Waterloo
Mascher
Mutter
Hancock
Palethorp
Second
Philip
Dillman
American
Bodine
Third
Galloway
Orianna
Fourth
Leithgow
Lawrence
Orkney
Fifth
Reese
Randolph
Fairhill
Sixth
Wendle
Marshall
Sheridan
Seventh
Beulah
Franklin
Perth
Eighth
Mildred
Darien
Schell
Ninth
Percy
Hutchinson
Delhi
Tenth
Alder
Warnock
Clifton
Eleventh
Jessup
Marvine
Sartain
Twelfth
Fawn
Camac
Iseminger

Thirteenth
Clarion
Juniper
Park avenue
Watts
Broad
Rosewood
Carlisle
Burns
Fifteenth
Hicks
Sydenham
Mole
Sixteenth
Bancroft
Smedley
Chadwick
Seventeenth
Colorado
Bouvier
Eighteenth
Cleveland
Gratz
Dorrance
Nineteenth
Garnet
Uber
Opal
Twentieth
Woodstock
Capitol
Lambert
Twenty-first
Norwood
Van Pelt
Beechwood
Twenty-second
Croskey
Hemberger
Twenty-third
Bonsall
Judson
Bucknell
Twenty-fourth
Ringgold
Taylor
Twenty-fifth
Stillman
Bambrey
Twenty-sixth
Bailey

SHEET ASPHALT PAVING of all kinds.

Taney
Chang
Twenty-seventh
Etting
Marston
Pennock
Twenty-eighth
Newkirk
Dover
Twenty-ninth
Hollywood
Myrtlewood
Thirtieth
Corlies
Stanley
Thirty-first
Napa
Patton
Thirty-second
Natrona
Douglass
Thirty-third
Spangler
Thirty-fourth
Shedwick
Warfield
Thirty-fifth
Harmony
Grove
Thirty-sixth
McAlpin
Thirty-seventh
DeKalb
Thirty-eighth
Lowber
Saunders
Thirty-ninth
State
Sloan
Fortieth
Wiota
Preston
Budd
Forty-first
Palm
Holly
Forty-second
St Marks
Brooklyn
Hutton
Forty-third
Pallas
Forty-fourth
Mica
Lex
Forty-fifth

Melville
Forty-sixth
June
Markoe
May
Forty-seventh
Moss
Forty-eighth
Fallon
Hanson
Forty-ninth
St. Bernard
Fiftieth
Farson
Fifty-first
Paxon
Fifty-second
Wilton
Fifty-third
Peach
Fifty-fourth
Conestoga
Sickels
Fifty-fifth
Allison
Fifty-sixth
Frazer
Fifty-seventh
Alden
Fifty-eighth
Wanamaker
Fifty-ninth
Redfield
Sixtieth
Edgewood
Sixty-first
Robinson
Sixty-second
Hirst
Felton
Wilkinson
Sixty-third
Gross
Sixty-fourth
Simpson
Sixty-fifth
Daggett
Sixty-sixth
Shields
Sixty-seventh
Sixty-eighth
* * * * *
Seventy-second
Lloyd
Seventy-third
* * * * *

RICHARDSON & ROSS, 30th & Race Sts.

EAST AND WEST STREETS, NORTH OF MARKET STREET

Market
Urbanna
Commerce
Filbert
Cuthbert
Walden
Arch
Appletree
Cherry
Quarry
Race
Spring
Florist
Summer
Winter
Vine
Pearl
Wood
Carlton
Callowhill
Shamokin
Willow
Pegg
Noble
Hamilton
Ralston
Buttonwood
Nectarine
Spring Garden
Monterey
Brandywine
Wilcox
Green
Clay
Mt. Vernon
Lemon
Wallace
North
Melon
Potts
Fairmount ave.
Olive
Perot
Meredith
Aspen
Folsom
Swain
Brown
Reno
Parrish
Myrtle
Ogden
Harmer
Westminster
Pennsgrove
Wyalusing

Hoopes
Laird
Poplar
Ellen
Laurel
Pollard
Wildey
George
Cambridge
Harper
Girard ave.
Walter
Stiles
Baltz
Cabot
Thompson
Seybert
Ingersoll
Kershaw
Master
Harlan
Sharswood
Media
Lansdowne
Hunter
Stewart
Jefferson
Nassau
Bolton
Redner
Oxford
Guest
Turner
Nicholas
Columbia ave.
Hollingsworth
Palmer
Eyre
Montgomery ave
Morse
Wilt
Euclid
Berks
Hewson
Arlington
Norris
Page
Fontain
Diamond
Edgley
Westmont
French
Susquehanna ave.
Colona
Fletcher
Nevada

ASPHALTUM BLOCKS and TILES.

SHRIVER, BARTLETT & CO. {ADJUSTMENTS COLLECTIONS}

Dauphin
 Dakota
 Gordon
 Arizona
York
 Boston
 Hagert
 Letterly
Cumberland
 Freedley
 Firth
 Sergeant
 Hazzard
Huntingdon
 Harold
 Albert
 Tucker
 Oakdale
Lehigh ave.
 Sterner
 Silver
 Seltzer
Somerset
 Rush
 Auburn
 William
Cambria
 Monmouth
 Birch
 Orleans
 Bellmore
 Stella
Indiana
 Mayfield
 Toronto
 Neff
 Elkhart
 Commissioner

Clearfield
 Clementine
 Lippincott
 Wishart
Allegheny ave.
 Hilton
 Madison
 Willard
Westmoreland
 Cornwall
 Wensley
 Thayer
Ontario
 Russell
 Estaugh
 Schiller
Tioga
 Atlantic
 Kingston
Venango
 Victoria
 Pacific
Erie ave.
 Airdrie
 Carey
Butler
 Archer
Pike
 McFerran
 Kerbaugh
Luzerne
 Henvis
 Ruffner
 Staub
 Dounton
 Juniata
Hunting Park ave.
 * * * * *

EAST AND WEST STREETS, SOUTH OF MARKET.

Market
 DeGray
 Ludlow
 Ranstead
Chestnut
 Ionic
 Gatzmer
 Sansom
 Moravian
Walnut
 Chancellor
 St James
 Locust
 Rittenhouse sq.
 Latimer
 Irving
 Manning

Spruce
 Cypress
 DeLancey
 Panama
Pine
 Waverly
 Addison
Lombard
 Gaskill
 Tryon
 Naudain
 Rodman
South
 Kater
Bainbridge
 Kenilworth
 Senate

RICHARDSON & ROSS, 30th & Race Sts.

Monroe
Pemberton
Fitzwater
Clymer
St Albans
Fulton
Catharine
Kauffman
Queen
Webster
Beck
Norfolk
Christian
Salter
Montrose
Hall
Carpenter
Mott
Kimball
League
Washington av
Alter
Peters
Ellsworth
Ernst
Annin
Federal
Manton
Ingram
Oakford
Latona
Titan
Wharton
Sears

Medina
Earp
Reed
Gerritt
Wilder
Dickinson
Greenwich
Cross
Tasker
Fernon
Mountain
Morris
Watkins
Pierce
Moore
McClellan
Sigel
Mifflin
Hoffman
Dudley
McKean
Emily
Mercy
Snyder av
Cantrell
Winton
Jackson
Tree
Daly
Wolf
Durfor
Fitzgerald
Ritner
* * * * * *

WEST PHILADELPHIA.

Hoffman av
Thole
Thomas av
Bremall
Whitby av
Malcolm
Hadfield
Willows av
Pentridge
Florence av
Beaumont
Warrington av
Windsor
Springfield av
Trinity
Chester av
Regent
Kingsessing av
Upland

Greenway av
Bicking
Yocum
Woodland av
Saybrook
Paschall av
Glenmore
Gray's av
Elmwood av
Dickens
Buist's av
Chelwynde
Dick's av
Guyer
Grover's av
Barrett
Lyons av
Brunswick

SHEET ASPHALT PAVING of all kinds.

Suffolk av	**Eastwick av**
Albertson	**Bartram av**
Gibson av	**Botanic av**
Haley	**Laycock av**

NORTH AND SOUTH STREETS EAST OF NORTH FRONT.

Front	**F**
Lee	Weymouth
Water	Custer
Swanson	Reach
A	**G**
Ella	Shelborne
Kip	**H**
B	Argyle
Ormes	**I**
Rosehill	Palmetto
Rutledge	Elsinore
C	**J**
Arbor	Lawndale
Boudinot	Bennington
Hurley	**K**
D	Claridge
Gransback	Howland
Rorer	**L**
Hartville	Dungan
E	Glendale

ALPHABETICAL LIST OF STREETS.

A.

A, N fr 2500 Ktn av to E Huntingdon. & fr E Lehigh av to Cheltenham av

ABBOTSFORD AV (Gtn & Falls), N E fr Scott's la to Morris, N of Apsley

ABIGAIL, E fr Coral to 2050 Trenton av, S of E Susq'ana av

ABINGTON AV (C Hill), E fr N 35th to Stenton av, N of Willow Grove av

ABIOS AV, S E fr Wash'n av to Hermit, bel Belmina

ACADEMY RD (Byberry), S W fr Gravel rd to Welsh rd

ACCOMAC PL, N W fr 311 Wildey, E of Marlborough

ACTON PL, S fr 1122 Pearl

ADAIR AV, E fr 453 N 13th

ADAMS, S E fr 2439 Ktn av to Moyer

ADAMS AV (Fkd), W fr 4058 Fkd av to Ktn & Olney turnpike

ADDISON, W fr 416 S 4th, E fr 417 & W fr 414 S 6th to S 9th, E & W fr S Alder, 412 S 12th to S Camac, E fr 415 S Juniper & W fr 422 S 16th to S 21st

AGATE, N E fr Tucker to Erie av, S E of Tulip

AGNES CT (Fkd), S fr 4117 Fkd av

AINSLEY (Falls), N E fr Cresson to Stokley, N of Bowman

AIRDRIE, W fr Lawrence to N 5th, Old York rd to N 13th & fr Park av to junc, 3800 N Broad & Gtn av

ALBANUS, W fr N 13th to Old York rd, N of Rockland

ALBERT, S E fr 2631 Ktn av to Emerald, S of Oakdale, E fr 2617 Martha to Cedar & fr Aramingo av to Salmon, N of E Huntingdon

RICHARDSON & ROSS, 30th & Race Sts.

ALBERT'S AV, S fr 1222 Palmer

ALBERTSON AV (Pville), S W of S 83d to S 88th, W of Suffolk av

ALDEN (W P), N fr Market, W of N 57th, Arch to Race & fr Media to Lansdowne av

ALDER (See N & S Alder)

ALFRED (Gtn), N fr 309 Penn to Coulter, bet Patton av & Newhall

ALGARD (Bln), N E fr Welsh rd, N W of Cottage

ALICE'S CT, N fr 1003 Sansom

ALLAIRE PL, W fr 2016 Howard

ALLEGHENY AV, W fr 3200 N Front to Schuy'l riv. (See also E Allegheny av)

ALLEGHENY SQ, 25th ward, Allegheny av, Almond, Willington & Belgrade

ALLEN, W fr N Front to 1037 Gtn av (See also E Allen)

ALLEN'S CT, N fr 927 Rodman

ALLEN'S LA (Gtn), S W fr 7300 Gtn av to Wiss av, W of Mt Airy av

ALLENGROVE (Fkd), S E fr Fkd av ab Harrison

ALLISON (W P) (See N & S Allison)

ALLISON LA (Roxb), S W fr 4552 Mitchell, S W of Krams av

ALMIRA PL, W fr 720 N Front

ALMOND, N fr 1331 E Susquehanna av to Moyer & fr E Huntingdon N to Edg & fr Ash to Brill, S E of Belgrade

ALPHA (Pville), W fr S 72d, S of Woodland av

ALSOP (M Town), W fr N 18th to N 19th, N of 65th, Av N

ALTER, W fr 1002 S Front, S S Reese to S Randolph, S 7th to S Franklin, 1118 S 8th to S Darien, 1114 S 12th, 1122 S 13th to W of S Broad, S 15th to S 16th, S 17th to S 18th, S 19th to S 24th, S 25th to S 27th & fr Gray's Ferry av to Schuy'l av, N of Ellsworth

AMBER, N E fr N Front & E Norris to E Lehigh av & fr 2101 E Somerset, thence to Fkd creek, E of Coral

AMBLER AV, N fr 1311 Cambridge

AMERICA, S fr Allegheny av to Lippincott, W of Del riv

AMERICAN (See N & S American)

AMERICAN PL, E fr 245 N 4th

AMOS PL, E fr 1411 Randolph

AMPHO AV (Myk), N W fr Hermit, bel Wissahickon av

ANANDALE PL, E fr 725 N 9th

ANDERSON (Gtn), E fr Gtn & N R R to Stenton av, N of Sullivan, thence to Somerville

ANDORRA AV (Roxb)(E fr Ridge av to Wiss Creek, S of county line

ANDREWS (Gtn), N fr Limekiln pike to Cheltenham av, E of Walnut la

ANDREWS LA (Pville), W fr Gibson av to Elmwood av, S of S 68th

ANN, S E fr 2991 Fkd av to Del riv

ANGORA (W P) S W fr S 59th to county line, W of Baltimore av

ANN'S PL, E fr 1317 S Hancock

ANNA (W P), N fr Race to Westminster av, N W of Columbia av & N 72d

ANNIN, W fr S Marshall to 1141 S 8th, 1156 S 9th to W of S 13th, 1150 S 16th to S 18th, 1138 S 19th to S 22d, S 25th to Gray's Ferry av & fr 1130 S 28th to Schuylkill av

APPLE (Myk), N W fr 124 Walnut la to Pensdale, ab Cresson

APPLETREE, W fr 116 N Front, 118 N 4th, E fr 115 N 8th, W fr 118 N 10th to N 11th, 112 N 12th to N Juniper, 118 N 15th to N 17th, 112 N 20th to N Beechwood & (W P) fr N 56th to W of Alden, N of Arch

APSLEY (Gtn), W fr Gtn av, S of Abbotsford av

ARAMINGO AV, N W fr Del riv to Duncan, S E of Memphis

ARBOR, N fr E Somerset to E Indiana & fr E • Ontario to E Tioga, E of C

ARCADIA, N E fr 2067 E Sergeant & fr Wheatsheaf la to Vici

ARCH, W fr 100 N Del av to Schuyl riv, fr N 32d to N 34th, & fr N 40th to City Line av

ARCHER (N Town), N fr Gtn av to Pike & S fr Ruffner to Butler, E of Blaine & (Gtn) fr Hansberry to Queen, S W of Morris

ARDMORE AV (C Hill), S fr Graver's la, bel Stenton av

ARENDEL (Torresdale), N W fr Del riv to Fkd av, N E of Linden av

ASPHALTUM BLOCKS and TILES.

ARGYLE AV (Lawndale), N E fr
Benner to Robbins, N of Oxford
Pike
ARIZONA, W fr N 9th to N 11th, N
25th to N 28th, & fr N 29th to N
33d, S of York (See also E Arizona)
ARLINGTON, W fr 1936 N Law-
rence, N 17th to N 18th, Ring-
gold to N 25th, N 30th to N
Patton & fr N 32d to N 33d, S
of Norris
ARMAND PL, W fr 712 N Marshall
ARMAT (Gtn), E fr 5601 Gtn av to
Morton
ARMSTRONG'S CT, N fr 1307 Ful-
ton, W of S Juniper
ARMSTRONG'S LA (Gtn), W fr
Stenton av to Bellfield, S of
Penn
ARROTT (Fkd), W fr 4738 Fkd av
to Asylum pike
ARTHUR (Hbg), N fr Van Horn to
Fairview, E of Hickory
ARTISAN, N fr 2802 E Norris to
Ball, E of Richmond
ASBURY TER (Oak La Sta), W fr
Cheltenham av to Oak la
ASH, S fr Mifflin to Del riv, E of
R R
ASH (Bdg), N W fr Richmond to
Fkd creek, S of Kirkbride
ASHANTEE (C Hill), N W fr Sun-
set to Bells Mill rd, W of Gtn av
ASHBURNER (Hbg), E of Fkd av
to Del riv, N of Pennypack creek
ASHLAND, N E fr Sepviva to
Stiles, W of Roxb
ASHMEAD (Gtn), N E fr 5201 Gtn
av, S E of Bringhurst
ASHTON PL, E fr 231 N 23d
ASHTON RD (Byberry)
ASHURST (W. P.), W fr Cobb's
creek to county line, S of Arch.
ASHWOOD (L'ville), S fr S 86th
to S 90th, E of Holstein
ASPEN, W fr 730 N 22d to P &
R R W & fr N 25th to W of N
26th, N of Fairmount av, & (W
P), fr N 34th to Haverford
ASTOR PL, W fr 804 N Front
ASYLUM RD (Fkd), N fr Adams to
Crescentville & Tacony Creek
ATKINSON'S RD (Byberry), E fr
Byberry pike to county line
ATLANTIC, W fr Dillman to Glen-
wood av, Mascher to Palethorp,
fr N 7th, 3512 N. 12th to Gtn av,
& fr N 17th to N 23d, S of Ve-
nango (See also E Atlantic)

ATLEE PL, W fr S Hancock, S
of Queen
AUBURN, W fr N 9th to N Hutch-
inson, 2812 N 12th to Park av, &
fr N Broad to Glenwood av (See
also E Auburn)
AUGUST (Fkd), N W fr Scatter-
good to Brill, N of James
AURANIA (Myk), S W fr Ridge av
to Eva, N W of Shawmont
AUSTIN PL, E fr 831 N American
AVENUE A (P'ville), S fr S 80th &
W of Cobb's creek
AVENUE C, E fr 323 New Market
AVENUE E (P'ville), W fr S 74th,
S of Elmwood av
AVENUE F (P'ville), W fr S 73d,
S of Buist's av
AVENUE G (P'ville), E fr S 87th
W of Welcome
AVENUE 36, S of Hoyt
AVENUE 37, S to Avenue 4500 S
(not opened).
AXE FACTORY RD (Bln), N W fr
Pennypack to Bln pike, E of Fox
Chase rd

B.

B, N fr Ktn av & Huntingdon to
Cheltenham av, E of A
BACH'S CT, N fr 1415 Race
BADEN, S fr Kater to 741 Bain-
bridge
BAILEY, N fr 2609 Parrish to Pop-
lar & fr 2625 Jefferson to Colum-
bia av
BAILEY PL, S fr 118 Catharine
BAILEY'S CT (Fkd), N fr 119 John
BAINBRIDGE, W fr 700 S Del av
to Schuylkill av
BAIRD'S CT (Fkd), S E fr 4117
Fkd av
BAKER (Myk), N W fr Gay to Du-
pont, N E of Cresson & fr Dupont
to Ripka, ab High
BAKER AL, N fr 529 De Lancey
BAKER'S CT, N fr 923 Palmer
BALDWIN (Myk), fr Silverwood to
Wilde, N of Green lya
BALFOUR, N fr E Allegheny av to
N Del av, N W of Caspar
BALL, E fr 2235 Richmond to Beach
BALL'S AV (Fkd), W fr 4436 Paul
BALL'S CT. W fr 964 N Front
BALLENGER AV, S fr 1112 Race
BALLOW'S LA, S E fr Yankee
Pt, Schuy'l to Penrose av, S W of
Driving Park

RICHARDSON & ROSS, 30th & Race Sts.

BALSAM PL, E fr 747 S 5th
BALSTON PL, N fr 251 Fulton
BALTIMORE AV (W P), S W fr S
  39th & Woodland av to Cobb's
  Creek
BALTZ, W fr 1236 N 30th
BAMBREY (See N & S Bambrey)
BANCROFT (Milestown) (See also
  N & S Bancroft)
BANEKER (Wiss), S fr Dawson to
  Osborn, E of Myk av
BANES (Bln), E fr Pennypack to
  Lott, N of Fulmore
BANK, S fr 230 Market to Chestnut
BANK AV, N fr Harmony ct to
  Stock Exchange pl, W of S 3d
BARBER'S ROW, N fr 1109 Melon
BARING (W P), W fr 334 N 31st to
  N 42d, N of Powelton av
BARKER'S PL, W fr 1022 Crease
  to Day
BARLOW PL, N fr 733 Pemberton
BARNES PL, E fr 1123 N Orianna
BARNHURST PL, N fr 1803 Francis
BARRETT AV, S fr S 83d to S
  88th, bet Grover's av & Lyon av
BARTON (Tacony), S fr Tacony to
  Wissino, N E of Tyson
BARTRAM'S AV (W P), S E fr
  Chester branch P & R R W at S
  47th to Bow creek
BARTRAM'S GARDEN (27th
  ward), S 53d to S 54th, Eastwick
  av & Schuy'l river
BASS (Gtn) N W fr 127 Phil El-
  lena to Pleasant, N E of Mus-
  grove
BATH, N fr 2867 William to Jenks,
  W of Brabant & (Frdg) Kirkbride
  to Reynolds, S E of Allen
BATTERSBY (Fkd), N E fr Bristol
  turnpike & Benner, E of Brous
BAXTER'S PL, S fr 428 Fitz-
  water
BAXTER'S PL, W fr 708 N Mar-
  shall
BAYNTON (Gtn), N W fr Shed-
  aker to Wister & fr Penn to
  Duval, E of Gtn av
BEACH N fr Willow to E Hunting-
  don, E of N Front
BEALE PL, N fr 1729 Ranstead
BEARD'S CT, W fr 1536 N 5th
BEAUMONT (W P), W fr 812 S
  48th to S 51st, & fr S 57th to S
  60th, N of Pentridge
BEAUMONT PL, N fr 107 Pegg

BEAVER, S fr Wiccacoe av to Gov-
  ernment av, W of East
BECK, W fr 846 S Swanson to S
  Hancock, & fr 842 S 2d & E fr
  S 5th, S of Queen
BEECHWOOD (See N & S Beech-
  wood)
BEEKMAN PL N fr 421 Green
BEGGARTOWN LA, E fr Schuy'l
  av, S of Curtin to Hollander's
  creek, W of S 20th
BEHAN'S PL, E fr 1311 Cadwalla-
  der
BELGRADE, N E fr 1401 Fkd av
  to E York, E Somerset to E Al-
  legheny av, thence to Herbert
  (Bdg), bet Almond & Gaul &
  (Fkd) fr Ash to Pratt, N W of
  Almond
BELL'S CT, r of 317 Spruce
BELLEVUE, N W fr 1751 Francis
  to Wylie, W of Cameron
BELLFIELD (Gtn), N fr Stenton
  av to Church la, W of Wingo-
  hocking, & fr Church la to Wal-
  nut la, E of Magnolia, thence N
  W to Chew & Wash'n
BELMORE AV, E fr 2967 Fkd av
  to Amber
BELMINA (Myk), W fr Hermit,
  bel Ampho av
BELMONT AV (W P), N fr Lan-
  caster av to City Line av, W of
  N 43d
BENCKERT'S AV (W P), W fr 3922
  Warren
BENEZET (C Hill), W fr P & R
  R R to N 26th, bet Mermaid av &
  Willow Grove av
BENNER (Voltown & Fkd), runs E
  fr Wentz farm reservoir along
  northern boundary North Cedar
  Hill Cemetery, Fkd, & (Wissino),
  W fr Del riv to Montg'y Co line,
  N E of Comly
BENNER'S AV, N fr 2829 Sus-
  q'ana av to Fletcher
BENNINGTON (Olney)
BENSALEM TURNPIKE (Byberry),
  E fr Bln & Somerton pike to Po-
  quessing Creek
BENSON AV (Fox Chase), S E fr
  E to H, S W of Strable
BERDAN (Gtn), N W fr Upsal, W
  of Gtn av
BERGES, E fr 2010 Amber to Tren-
  ton av

SHEET ASPHALT PAVING of all kinds.

BERKLEY (Gtn), N fr Wissahickon av to Gtn av, N W of Robert's av

BERKS, W fr 1864 N Front to N Broad, N 16th to N 25th & fr Ridge av to the Park, ab Montg'y av & (W P), fr N 52d to N 57th, & fr N 62d to N 69th, ab Montg'y av

BERKSHIRE (Bdg), S E fr Almond to Richmond, N E of Ruan & (Fkd), fr Tackawanna to Torresdale av, S of Church

BERMUDA (Fkd), N fr Fkd creek, S of Cambridge

BERNARD'S CT., W fr 776 S 2d

BERRY PL, S fr 908 Locust

BERRY RD (Byberry)

BERTRAND PL, W fr 1248 Cadwallader

BETHLEHEM PIKE (O Hill), N E fr Gtn av & Summit to county line

BEULAH (See N & S Beulah)

BEVANS CT, N fr 227 Wash'n av

BEVERLY PL, N fr 827 Bainbridge

BICKAM'S CT, W fr 614 S Front

BICKING (Roxb), N W fr Gowen av, S of Wash'n

BIGLER, W fr Del riv to Schuy'l riv 2900 S

BIRCH, S fr Stiles, E of N 27th

BIRCH, W fr N Hancock to Palethorp, N. American to N 3d, N 8th to N 9th, & fr N 15th to N Sydenham, N of Cambria (See also E. Birch)

BIRKWOOD (Bln), N E fr Murray to Lott, S of Duncan

BLABON (N Town), N fr Hunting Park av to Roberts av, N E of Schuyler

BLACK HORSE AL, W fr 24 S Front to S 2d

BLACKSON AV (Olney)

BLADEN'S CT, N fr 117 Cherry

BLAINE (N Town), N fr Hunting Park av to Ruffner, W of Archer

BLAIR, N fr 15 Oxford to Palmer, Montg'y av to Berks & S & N fr Norris to Trenton av, W of Fkd av

BLAVIS, W fr N 15th to N 18th, N of Cayuga

BLEDISLOE PL, W fr 936 N Marshall

BLEIGH, S E fr 2d st pk n Township line rd

BLIGHT'S LA, W fr S Front, bel av 35, S

BLINN'S CT, W fr 824 N 4th

BLUE GRASS RD (Byberry), W fr Red Lyon rd, ab Decatur rd

BODINE (See N & S Bodine)

BOILEAU (Bln), S E fr Meeting House rd to Bustleton pike

BOLIVIA PL, E fr 249 N 11th

BOLTON, W fr 2112 Ridge av to N 25th, N of Jefferson

BONITZ (N Town), W fr Wayne S of Bristol

BONSALL. (See N & S Bonsall)

BOONE (Myk), N W fr Markle to Mallory, S W of Terrace, Jamestown to Levering & fr Green la to Leverington av, N E of Silverwood

BORBECK (Fox Chase), N W fr 2d st pk, S of Loney

BOSTON, W fr N 7th to N 10th, Park av to N Broad, N 15th to N Sydenham & fr N 20th to N 21st, N of York (See also E Boston)

BOTANIC AV (W P), S W fr S 48th to S 79th, E of Bartram av

BOTT (N Town), N W fr 3906 N Broad to Lycoming

BOUDINOT, N fr 2754 Ktn av to Ontario, E of C

BOUVIER. (See N & S Bouvier)

BOWER PL, W fr 818 N Hancock to N 2d

BOWERS, N E fr 811 Perkiomen, W of N 17th

BOWER'S CT, E fr 941 Alder

BOWERY AV (O Hill), N fr Hartwell av to Graver's la

BOWERY PL, W fr 338 S Hicks

BOWLING'S CT, E fr 419 S 10th

BOWMAN (Falls), N E fr Cresson to Indian Queen la, N of Crawford

BOWMAN AV (W P) N W fr N 51st & Pearl

BOX GROVE AV (Hbg), W fr Rhawn to Holmesburg, E of Montague

BOYER (Gtn), N W fr Church la to Gtn av, E of Chew & (Mt Airy), fr Mt Pleasant av to Roumfort av

BRABANT, N fr Allegheny av to Kingston, E of Bath

BRACELAND'S CT, W fr 916 S Front

BRADDOCK, N fr 2011 E Huntingdon to E Lehigh av, 2034 E Clearfield W of Fkd av, Hart la S E of Emerald, & fr E Elkhart to E Tioga, W of Fkd av

BRANCH PL, E fr 221 N 3d

RICHARDSON & ROSS, 30th & Race Sts.

BRANCHTOWN PIKE (Gtn), continuation of Mill, N E fr Mill & Boyer to Branchtown

BRANDYWINE, W fr 530 N 7th to N Franklin, N 8th to N 9th, 534 N 10th to N 12th, 1220 Ridge av to N 13th, N 23d to Judson, N 24th to N 25th & (W P) N 23d to Spg Garden & fr N 40th to N 42d, N of Spg Garden

BREAD, N fr 227 Arch to Race & S fr 220 Winter

BREINTNALL PL, E fr 525 S 5th

BREWERY LA (Falls) S fr 149 Midvale av

BREWSTER AV (W P) S W fr S 77th, S E of Bartram's av

BRIDE PL, N fr 1211 Hamilton

BRIDGE (Fkd & Bdg), S E fr Fkd av to Del riv, S E of Cedar Hill Cemetery

BRIDGET (Wiss), W fr Hermit to Walnut la, S of Wiss av

BRIGHT (Fkd), N W fr Walker to Drexel & (Tacony), Wissinoming to Tacony, S W of Princeton

BRILL (Fkd & Bdg), N fr Edmund to Cottage, & Charles to Fkd av, James to Elwyn & fr Garden to Almond, N E of Bridge

BRINGHURST (Gtn), E fr 5235 Gtn av to Gtn R R & fr Archer to Laurens

BRISTOL (Bdg), E fr 4257 Richmond & (N Town) fr Fkd creek to Del riv, bel Cayuga

BRISTOL PIKE (Wissinoming)

BRISTOL PL E fr 615 S American

BRISTOW PL, E fr 621 Mascher

BROAD (See N & S Broad)

BROMLEY LA (Fkd), N E fr 2143 Church

BROOKS AV (W P), W fr N 54th to N 55th, N of Westminster av

BROOKS CT, S fr 1630 South to Kater

BROOKLYN (W P), N fr Haverford to 4221 Westminster av, & S fr Spruce to Pine, W of S 42d

BROOKLYN PL (W P), W fr 718 Brooklyn

BROOMALL AV (W P), N E fr S 53d to Baltimore av, N of Whitby av

BROUS (Fkd), N fr Benner, W of Battersby

BROWN, W fr 800 N Del av to Francis, N 19th to Penna av,

Park boundary; thence W fr N 36th, ab Aspen to Haverford

BROWN'S CT, W fr Chase pl, r 2306 Noble

BRUNNER, W fr 4218 Gtn av to Clarissa

BRUNSWICK (P'ville), W fr S 83d to S 88th, S E of Lyons av

BRUNSWICK PL, N fr 321 Pemberton

BRYAN (Mt Airy), N fr Allen's la, N of Mower

BRYANT (Gtn), N fr Mt Pleasant av to Durham, W of Gtn av

BRYN MAWR AV (W P), W fr Penna R R, N of Merion av

BUCHANAN PL, E fr 311 S Philip

BUCK RD, S E fr S 10th & Jackson to Old 2d st rd

BUCKINGHAM PL, S fr 236 Poplar

BUCKINGHAM PL (W P), N fr Locust, W of S 44th

BUCKIUS, W fr 3900 Fkd av to Ktn av, N of Butler & (Bdg), N fr Richmond to Fkd creek, bel Ash

BUCKNELL (See N & S Bucknell)

BUDD (W P), N fr 4065 Powelton av to Wallace, Aspen to Brown, & fr Ogden to Westminster av, E of N 41st

BUENA VISTA AV (P'ville)

BUIST'S AV (W P), S W fr S 59th & Gibson av to County line

BUIST'S CT, S fr 1214 Fitzwater

BUMMERSCHEIM CT, W fr 1730 N 8th to N Darien

BUNKER'S LA (Hbg), E fr Fkd av, N of Mill

BUNTING AV, E & W fr 136 Marston, N of Cherry

BURCHELL'S CT, E fr 835 S 3d

BURGESS PL, W fr 1224 E Columbia av

BURKE AV (Fox Chase), W fr Ktn & Oxford turnpike, S of School House la

BURLEIGH, N W fr E Girard av to Moyer, S W of E Norris

BURLING AV (Byberry), N fr Bensalem pike, W of Meeting House rd

BURLINGTON PL, N fr 235 Fitzwater

BURNS, N fr 1441 Cherry to Race, Brown to Parrish, Stiles to Thompson & fr Clearfield to Allegheny av, W of N Froad

ASPHALTUM BLOCKS and TILES.

SHRIVER, BARTLETT & CO. {ADJUSTMENTS COLLECTIONS

BURNSIDE (Myk), N E fr Apple to Tower & fr Myk av to Lauriston, N W of Walnut la

BURR'S AV, N fr 1419 Wood to Carlton

BURWICK PL, E fr 725 Mascher

BUSTLETON & SOMERTON PIKE (Bln), N fr Bridge to Bln

BUTLER, W fr N Front to Roberts av, ab Erie av (See also E Butler)

BUTTON (Gtn), S fr Godfrey to Spencer av, W of N 20th

BUTTONWOOD, W fr 520 N 2d to N 20th & fr 518 N. 23d to N 26th

BUTZ AV, N fr 209 Noble

BUTZ ROW, E fr 491 N American

BYRON PL, E fr 1339 Gtn av

C.

C, N fr 2722 Ktn av to Cheltenham av, E of B

CABOT, W fr 1238 N 12th to N 13th, 1242 N 15th to N 17th, N 18th to N 19th, N Taney to N 28th & fr N 30th, ab Girard av (See also E Cabot)

CADWALLADER, N W fr Girard av, W of N 2d to Berks, 2228 N 6th to Dauphin, fr 2426 N 8th to N 9th & fr 2516 N 9th to N of Huntingdon, E of Ctn av

CALIFORNIA PL, N fr 1311 Rodman

CALLOWHILL, W fr 400 N Del av to Schuy'l riv

CALUMET (Falls), S W fr Ridge av to Schuy'l riv & E fr 4135 Ridge av to Conrad, N W of Stanton

CALVIN PL, E fr 809 N 7th

CAMAC, (See N & S Camac)

CAMBRIA, W fr 2900 N Front to Ridge av (See also E Cambria)

CAMBRIDGE, W fr N Bodine to N Lawrence, N 5th to N Marshall, 964 N 7th, 926 N 12th to N Watts, N Carlisle to N 18th, N 19th to Corinthian av & fr N 27th to Penna av & (W P) fr N 38th to N 42d, S of Girard av

CAMBRIDGE (Fkd), N & E fr Roxb to Pratt, S of Stiles

CAMERON, W fr 1735 Francis to Vineyard, S of Perkiomen

CANAL, S E fr Allen to Del riv, S of Richmond

CANAL (Myk), N W fr Lock av, W of Main

CANDIA PL, S fr 516 Fairmount av

CANTMAN PL, W fr 678 N 11th

CANTON (Myk), N W fr 4610 Umbria to Wright

CANTRELL, W fr S 3d, fr 2116 S 5th to S 12th, & fr S 16th to S Chadwick, S of Snyder av

CANTRELL'S CT, W fr 1028 S 2d

CAPITOL (See N & S Capitol)

CARLEON, N fr Ontario to Erie av, W of Del riv

CAREY, W fr N Lawrence to N 5th, S of Butler

CARLISLE (See N & S Carlisle)

CARLTON, W fr 328 N Del av to N Front, N Mascher to N 2d, 336 N American, 358 N Orianna to N 4th, N 9th to Ridge av, N 10th to N 23d & E fr N 24th, S of Callowhill

CARPENTER, W fr 936 S Front to Schuy'l riv

CARPENTER (Gtn), W fr 6000 Gtn av to Wiss av

CARPENTER'S CT, S fr 320 Chestnut (now Congress pl)

CARR AV (C Hill), N E fr N 35th to N 30th, W of Cresheim creek

CARRIGAN CT, W fr 532 S Taney

CARROLL AV, S fr 1208 Cambridge

CARROLL AV (W P), W fr S 43d to S 46th, S of Pine

CARSELL AV, E fr 719 N Broad

CARSON (Myk), N E fr 4427 Main to Green la

CARSWELL (Gtn), N W fr Haines to Mechanic, N E of Baynton

CARSWELL PL, E fr 1109 S Marshall

CARUTH PL, S fr 412 Wharton

CARWITHIAN (Bln), S E fr Meeting House rd to Starkey, S of Gregg

CASPER, N fr E Allegheny av to Del riv, W of Carbon

CASTLE AV, W fr 1726 S 13th to S 15th

CASTNER AV, W fr 934 N Orkney

CASTOR RD (Fkd), N fr Oxford rd to Fox Chase rd, N E of Duncan rd

CATHARINE, W fr 800 S Del av to Gray's Ferry av ab Christian, & fr S Bambrey to Schuyl av & (W P) fr Baltimore av ab S 49th to Del County line

CAYUGA, W fr N 19th to Gratz & E fr Roberts av to Fkd creek, ab Bristol

RICHARDSON & ROSS, 30th & Race Sts.

CEDAR, N E fr 1541 Vienna to Fkd creek, E of Memphis

CEDAR (Fkd), N E fr Wilmot to Bridge, E of Fkd av

CEDAR AV (W P), W fr S 46th, to S 52d, S of Baltimore av

CEMETERY AV (Gtn), E fr Cresheim rd to Haines, N of Stenton

CEMETERY LA (W P), N W fr Woodland av to Mt Moriah Cemetery, S W of S 52d

CEMETERY RD (Somerton), N fr Bln pk to P & R Rw

CENTENNIAL AV, W fr 232 N Front

CENTRAL PL, W fr 256 N 5th

CHADWICK. (See N & S Chadwick)

CHADWICK PL, W fr 858 N 4th

CHAMBERS AV, S fr 2026 Callowhill

CHAMPLOST (Gtn), E fr N 19th to Vankirk, S of Spencer

CHANCELLOR, W fr 220 Dock to S 3d, fr 202 S Darien, S Hutchinson, W of S 9th, S 10th to S Clifton, S Marvine to S 11th, S 12th to S 18th, S 20th to W of S 21st, E fr S 22d, W fr S Bonsall to 207 S 24th, & (W P) E & W fr S 32d to 209 S 33d & E & W fr S 38th to S 40th, S of Walnut

CHANDLER'S CT, E fr 1019 E Eyre to E Montg'y av

CHANG, N fr 2631 Poplar to Girard av & S fr Stiles, W of N 26th

CHAPELCROFT (Bln), N E fr Murray to Lott, S of Hoff

CHARLES (Fkd), N E fr Harrison to Longshore, E of Mulberry

CHARLES (Hbg), E fr Decatur to Rhawn, S of Fkd av

CHARLES PL, W & N fr Willow, ab Percy

CHARLES ROW, N fr Clearfield, W of N 21st

CHATHAM, N fr E Somerset to E Erie av, E of Cedar

CHATHAM PL, W fr 502 N Randolph

CHELTEN AV (Gtn), W fr 5700 Gtn av to Wiss av. (See also E Chelten av)

CHELTENHAM & WILLOW GROVE PIKE, continuation of Old York rd, 22d Wd

CHELTENHAM AV (O Hill), S E fr Cresheim av to city line

CHELWYNDE AV (P'ville), W fr S 62d & fr S 84th to Island rd, S of Buist av

CHENANGO, E fr 1113 Sophia to 1113 N Hancock, N of Wildey

CHEROKEE AV (C Hill), N fr Mermaid av, W of N 34th

CHERRY, W fr 126 N Front to N 2d, & fr N American to Schuy'l riv & (W P) W fr 118 N 32d to N 34th, N 38th to Saunders av & fr N 55th to N 58th, S of Race

CHESTER AV (W P), W fr S 41st to Cobb's creek, S E of Springfield av

CHESTNUT, W fr 100 S Del av to Schuyl riv, thence W to Del County line

CHESTNUT AV, E fr 7 N Clifton

CHESTNUT HILL AV (O Hill), E fr N 32d & Spg House pike, ab Rex

CHEW (Gtn), N E fr Stenton av to Mt Airy av, W of Boyer

CHEW (Olney), W fr Clinton, N of Olney av

CHEYENNE (W P), N fr Lancaster av, W of N 60th

CHRISTIAN, W fr 900 S Del av to Schuylkill riv, & (W P) from Baltimore av at S 53d to Del County line

CHURCH, W fr 18 N Front to N 3d

CHURCH (Fkd), N W fr Tacony to Adams, S of Unity

CHURCH LA (Gtn) N E fr Gtn av, ab E Coulter to N 20th, N of Champlost

CHURCH LA (P'ville), N fr Woodland av, E of S 70th

CINNAMINSON (Myk), N E fr Umbria to Ridge av, N of Lemonte

CITY AV, N E fr Del Co line to Del riv bet Phila & Mont'g Cos

CLAIBORN, N fr 1220 Plum, E of Richmond

CLAPIER (Gtn), S W fr Baynton, N of Shedaker, E fr 4031 Gtn av to Wakefield & fr Morris to Township line rd, E of Manheim (See also E Clapier)

CLARION (See N & S Clarion)

CLARISSA, N fr Hunting Park av to Roberts av, W of Wayne

CLARISSA PL, W fr 542 Linden

3

SHEET ASPHALT PAVING of all kinds.

CLARK (Bln), E fr Pennypack to Lott, S of Hoff

CLARK'S AV, S fr 418 Button-wood

CLARK'S PARK (27th ward), S 43d to S 44th, bet Baltimore av & Chester av

CLARK'S PL, S fr 2010 & 2016 Wood

CLARKSON AV (Gtn), E fr Stenton av, N of Somerville av to Cemetery, W of Cedar Hill Cemetery

CLAWGES CT, N fr 513 Sumner

CLAY, W fr 608 N 11th to Ridge av & fr N 21st to N 22d, N of Green

CLEARFIELD, W fr 3100 N Front to Ridge av (See also E Clearfield)

CLEARVIEW AV (Gtn), fr 518 E Walnut la to P & R Rw

CLEMATIS AV, S fr 114 Christian

CLEMENTINE, W fr N 13th to Park av & fr 3124 N 29th to N 30th, N of Clearfield
(See also E Clementine)

CLERMONT (W P), E fr N 45th to Lex, N of Wallace

CLEVELAND (B Town), N fr Lime-kiln pk, E of Mill
(See also N & S Cleveland)

CLIFFORD, W fr N 24th to N 25th, & fr N 30th to N 33d, N of Columbia av

CLIFFORD'S AL, W fr 28 N Del av to N Front

CLIFTON (See N & S Clifton)

CLINTON, W fr S 9th to 11th, S of Spruce

CLIVEDEN (Gtn), S W fr Emlen to Belmina, S E of Upsal
(See also E Cliveden)

CLOUD (Fkd), S & N fr Church to Waln, E of Orchard & N E fr Plum to Wilmot, E of Mulberry

CLOVER, W fr 24 S 11th to S 13th

CLYMER, W fr 774 S Swanson to W of S Front, E & W fr 756 S 6th to S 8th, 746 S Juniper to S Watts, E fr S 15th, W fr 746 S 20th to S 24th

COAL AV, E fr 337 S 26th

COGGSHELL AV (Gtn), S fr Rittenhouse, ab Green

COHEN'S CT, N fr 431 Fitzwater

COKE PL, N fr 417 Carpenter

COLEBAUGH (Fkd), N E fr Bristol turnpike, E of Battersby

COLEMAN (W P), S W fr Vine to Cobb's creek, W of Malvern

COLLEGE AV (See N & S College av)

COLLINS, N fr 2153 E Dauphin to E York, E Cumberland to E Lehigh av, E Clearfield to Elkhart, & fr E Allegheny av to E Tioga

COLLINS CT, W fr 400 N 23d

COLLOM (Gtn), N fr 5201 Gtn av to Armstrong

COLLS AV, N fr 607 Webster, W of Passy'k av

COLONA, W fr 2210 N Howard to N Hancock, 2228 N 10th, to N 12th, W fr N 28th, & fr N 30th to N 31st, N of Susq'ana av

COLONIAL TER (Gtn), W fr Morris to Wiss av, ab Price

COLORADO (See N & S Colorado)

COLUMBIA AV, W fr 1612 Fkd av to N 33d, & (W P), N W fr N 41st & Girard av to Cobb's creek, S of Parkside av, thence fr W Park to County line
(See also E Columbia av)

COLWELL (Gtn), N fr 115 Haines to Mechanic

COMLY (Fkd), E fr G to Del riv, N of Van Kirk

COMLY RD (Byberry), N W fr Academy rd, S E of Red Lion rd

COMMERCE, W fr N 4th to N 7th, 17 N 9th, E fr 19 & W fr 20 N 10th, 22 N 12th to N Juniper, 14 N 17th to N 22d, & (W P) W fr N 57th to N 58th, N of Market

COMMISSIONER, W fr N 6th to N 7th, & fr N 34th to N 35th, N of Indiana
(See also E Commissioner)

CONARD'S CT, N fr 1623 Melon

CONARROE (Myk), N E fr 4419 Main to Cresson, S E of Canton, 4417 Baker to Silverwood, E fr Myk av to Ridge av, N of Lyceum av & fr Ridge av to Magdalena, S of Dupont

CONCORD (Gtn), N W fr 5 Harvey, S W of Gtn av

CONCORD PL, N fr 223 Fulton

CONCORDIA AV, N fr 229 Fulton

CONESTOGA (W P)
(See N & S Conestoga)

CONGRESS PL (was Carpenter's ct), S fr 320 Chestnut

CONLIN'S CT, N fr 1325 Cambridge

CONROW CT, N fr 105 Chenango

RICHARDSON & ROSS, 30th & Race Sts.

CONSHOHOCKEN (W P), fr W side Schuylkill riv to City line av

CONVENT AV (Torresdale)

COOPER, N fr Sarah to Shackamaxon, N W of Beach, E Clearfield to E Venango, W of Bath, & (Bdg) fr Jenks to Kirkbride, S of Garden

COPE'S AL, W fr 136 S Del av

CORA (Gtn), E fr Stenton av to N 20th, N of Godfrey av

CORAL, N E fr 2101 N Front to E Cambria, Ann to E Clearfield, E Westmoreland to E Venango, & fr Wheatsheaf la to Vici, E of Fkd av

CORINTHIAN AV, N fr Fairmount av to Girard av, W of N 20th

CORLIES, N E fr Oxford to Glenwood av, 3015 Berks to Arlington, Ridge av to Susq'ana av, W of N 30th & fr 3017 York to Cumberland

CORNELIUS (Gtn), N W fr Johnson to Sharpnack, N E of Stenton av

CORNWALL, W fr N 5th to Fairhill, N of Westmoreland (See also E Cornwall)

CORWIN PL, W fr 312 N Front

COSGROVE (Gtn), S W fr Baynton, N W of High

COTTAGE (Fkd & Hbg), E fr Harrison to Ashburner, N of Jackson

COTTAGE (Gtn), N E fr Musgrove to Chew, ab E Walnut la

COTTAGE AV (N Town), N fr 2101 Hunting Park av to P & R Rw

COTTAGE LA (Gtn), E fr Stenton av, N of Clarkson av

COTTMAN (Tacony), N fr Del riv to County line, E of St Vincent av

COTTON (Myk), N E fr 4319 Main, S W of Grape

COULTER (Gtn), S W fr 5400 Gtn av to Wiss av (See also E Coulter)

COURTLAND (Gtn), E fr Gtn R R to O, N of Wingohocking

COURTLAND PL, W fr 306 Mascher

COWDEN (Bln), N E fr Welsh rd to Lott, S of Clark

COWPERTHWAIT PL, E fr 319 Mascher

COZZEN'S PL, W fr 934 Mascher

CRAIG (Hbg), N E fr Mill to Solly, W of Fkd av

CRAIG AV, N fr 1225 Shackamaxon

CRANMER (Pville), S W fr S 78th, S 80th, N W of Buists av

CRAWFORD (Falls), N E fr 4101 Ridge av to Wiss av

CREASE, N fr 253 Richmond to Belgrade

CREFELDT AV (C Hill) N W fr C Hill av, S of Gtn av

CRESCENT PL (W P), N fr 5011 Master

CRESHEIM AV (C Hill), S fr Chel tenham av to Cresheim rd, E of Mermaid av

CRESHEIM RD (Gtn), N W fr Carpenter to Cresheim creek, N E of Quincy

CRESSON (Falls), N fr Scott's la, E of P & N R & N W fr Ridge av (at Wiss sta.) to Paoli av

CRESSWELL (Falls), S fr 137 Midvale av, S of Norristown R R

CRESTLINE AV (W P), N E fr George's av, W boundary line of W Park

CRISPIN, N E fr Napfle & Ryan to Solly, N of Leon

CRITTENDEN (Gtn), N W fr Stenton av, ab Anderson

CROOKED BILLET, W fr 22 S Del av to S Water

CROOKED PL, E fr 467 Mascher

CROSKEY (Sec N & S Croskey)

CROSS, W fr 1522 Moyam'g av to S 6th, 1526 S 8th to Passy'k av & fr 1530 S 21st to Pt Breeze av

CROTHERS (Olney), N fr Tabor av, W of Clinton

CROTHER'S AV (Pville), S W fr S 86th to S 90th, E of Ashwood av

CROWSON (Gtn), N fr Hortter to Pleasant, W of Chew

CRYSTAL AV, E fr 211 N 2d

CUBAN PL, S fr 114 Poplar

CULVERT, N E fr 453 Poplar to N Orianna, thence E to 1014 Allen, & fr Emerald to Cedar, S of E Westmoreland

CUMBERLAND, W fr 2500 N Front to Glenwood av, W of N 20th, & fr Sedgley av & N 22d to N 31st (See also E Cumberland

CUNARD, S W fr Newland, N W of Dearnley

CUNNINGHAM AV, S fr 1112 Federal to Latona

ASPHALTUM BLOCKS and TILES.

CURTIN, W fr Del riv to Schuylkill riv, 3200 S

CUSCADEN'S CT, S fr 426 Fitzwater

CUSTER, N E fr E Clearfield to E Allegheny av, W of Ktn av

CUSTOM HOUSE PL, S fr Chestnut to Sansom, facing Custom House, W of S 4th

CUTHBERT, W fr 44 N Front to W of 50 N 2d, 34 N 5th to N 6th, E fr 43 N 7th, W fr N 9th, E fr 41 N 10th, E fr 43 N 11th, W fr 44 N 12th to N 23d & (W P) N W fr Filbert to Saunders av & fr N 32d to Lancaster av, S of Arch

CYPRESS, W fr 316 S 3d to S 7th, S 9th to S Marvine, 308 S 12th to S Broad, E fr 313 S 17th, W fr S 18th to S 19th, S 20th to S 25th, S of Spruce

D.

D, N fr 2800 Ktn av to Cheltenham av

DAGGETT (W P), N fr Market to Callowhill, W of N 65th

DAKOTA, W fr N 9th to N 11th, N 25th to N 26th & fr N 30th to Natrona, N of Dauphin (See also E Dakota)

DALKEITH, W fr Wayne to Pulaski av, N of Bristol

DALY, W fr Del riv to S 5th, S 7th to W of S 9th, & fr S 10th to S 13th, S of Tree

DALY'S CT, N fr 1339 Olive

DANIEL (Blue Bell Hill), N W fr Hermit to Walnut la, W of Wiss av

DANIEL PL, N fr 1339 Earl

DARIEN (See N & S Darien)

DARK RUN LA (Fkd), S E fr Hartshorne rd to Del riv, N of Olney av

DARLING PL, S fr 224 Willow

DARRAGH'S CT, E fr 233 N Watts

DARRAGH'S CT, W fr 418 S 12th

DAUPHIN, W fr 2262 N Front to N 33d. (See also E Dauphin)

DAVIS (Myk), N E fr Cresson to 4031 Boone, N W of Dexter

DAVIS AV, E fr 147 N 8th

DAVIS' AV, S fr 604 Fairmount av

DAVIS CT, W fr 520 N 5th to N Randolph

DAVIS' PL, N fr 1235 Bainbridge to Kater

DAWSON (Myk), N E fr Cresson to Ridge av, S W of Harvey

DAY, N E fr E Girard av to E Thompson & fr Richmond to Beach, E of Shackamaxon

DEAGEN PL, E fr 619 Hope

DEAL (Fkd), W fr Ktn av to Leiper, along N side Fkd creek, S of Adams

DEAL AV, S fr 1650 E Eyre

DEAN'S AV, W fr 1238 Crease to Day

DEARNLEY (Roxb), W fr Ridge av to Main, N of Shawmont av

DECATUR (Hbg), E fr Rowland av to Mill, S Rhawn

DECATUR RD (Byberry), S W fr Byberry rd to Red Lion rd, N of Academy rd

DEDAKER (Bln), E fr Pennypack to Lott, N of Tomlinson

DE GRAY, W fr S Del av to S Water, S of Market, E fr 7 S 10th, & fr 13 S 17th

DE KALB (W P) (See N & S De Kalb)

DE LANCEY, W fr 326 S. Front to S 4th, 326 S 5th to S 8th, 332 S Marvine, 318 S Broad to S 15th, E fr 325 S 16th, W fr 314 S 17th S 22d, S 23d to S 26th & (W P) S W fr S 38th to S 40th & fr S 59th to S 60th, S of Spruce

DELAWARE AV (See N & S Del av)

DELHI (See N & S Delhi)

DELL (N Town), N W fr McFerran to E of N Broad, S of Roxb

DELMAR (Myk & Roxb), N E fr Smick to Ridge av, N of Fountain

DENK'S CT, E fr 823 N 3d

DENNEY PL, W fr 830 S Hancock

DENNIE (Gtn), W fr 4360 Gtn av to Schuyler, S of Roberts av

DEPOT (C Hill), E fr C Hill & Bethlehem turnpike, S of C Hill av

DERINGER'S AV, E fr 1541 N Front

DESILVER'S CT, S fr 428 Walnut

DE SOTO PL, N fr 1227 Summer to Winter

RICHARDSON & ROSS, 30th & Race Sts.

DEVEREAUX (Fkd), N fr Benner, E of G to beyond Bristol turnpike & (Marburg)

DE VICTOR (Hbg), S fr Ditman to Torresdale av, N of Solly

DEVON (Gtn), N W fr Stenton av to Chelten av, S W of Sprague

DEXTER (Myk), N W fr Seville to Walnut la & fr Roxb to Green la, S of Myk av

DIAMOND, W fr 2100 N Front to Park boundary

DIAMOND CT, S fr 620 South

DICKENS AV (P'ville), S W fr S 62d to S 63d & fr S 76th to S 78th, E of Elmwood av

DICKERSON'S CT, N fr 1343 Olive

DICKINSON, W fr 1500 S Del av to S 25th & fr S 33d W

DICKINSON SQ (1st ward), Tasker to Morris, Moyam'g av to S 4th

DICKS AV (W P), S W fr Gibson av to Island rd, ab S 61st

DILIGENT AV, N fr 915 Hamilton

DILKS CT, S fr 904 Wood

DILLMAN, N fr Page to Fontain & fr 721 Cuterio to Glenwood av, E of N 3d

DINGLER'S CT, S fr 116 Vanhorn

DISCOUNT PL, W fr 32 N 6th

DISSTON (Hbg), S E fr Bristol pk to Del riv, E of Longshore

DISSTON PARK (35th ward), Phila & Trenton R R, Princeton, Magee & Keystone

DISTRICT PL, E fr 313 N 10th

DITMAN (Fkd), N E fr Oxford to Meadow, N of Torresdale av, thence to Longshore, Tacony, S of Tackawanna

DITMAN (Hbg), S fr Maple av, E of Cottage av

DIVINITY PL (W P), S fr 5016 Greenway av to Woodland av

DIVISION, W fr 410 N 11th to N 12th

DIVISION (Falls), E fr Conrad ab Bowman

DIXON'S LA (Cedar Grove)

DOBSON (Falls), N fr Midvale av, W of N 37th

DOBSON'S ROW (Falls), E fr N 35th, N of Allegheny av

DOCK, N W fr S Del av ab Spruce to S 3d, N of Walnut

DOMAN'S PL, N fr 235 Christian

DOMINGO PL, S fr 1623 Lombard

DOMINO (Roxb), N E fr Schuy'l riv to Ridge av, N of Paoli av

DONNELLY'S CT, S fr 1816 Naudain to South

DONNELLY'S CT, W fr 826 N Hancock

DONNELLY'S PL, N fr 137 Winter

DORRANCE, S fr Fitzwater to Catharine, Ellsworth to Federal, Wharton to Earp, Dickinson to Tasker, Morris to Moore & fr McKean to Snyder av, W of S 18th

DORRITT, W fr N 18th, S of Cayuga

DORSET (Gtn), N W fr Chew to Boyer, & fr Pickering to Cheltenham av, ab Phil Ellena

DOUGHERTY'S CT, N fr 107 Vine

DOUGHERTY'S CT, S fr 1140 Olive

DOUGHERTY'S CT, S fr 514 South to Kater

DOUGLAS, N fr Susq'ana av to Diamond, & fr York to Huntingdon, & (W P), N fr Haverford, W of N 32d

DOUGLAS AV, S fr 1230 Brown

DOUNTON (N Town), E fr 4168 Gtn av & W to Wayne, S of Juniata

DOVER (See N & S Dover)

DOVER'S CT, S fr 914 Poplar

DOYLE'S CT, E fr 605 S 3d

DRAIN, S fr 2806 Oakdale

DRAYSON PL, N fr 1137 Pine

DRAYTON, W fr 1232 S. Philip to S American

DREER, S E fr 2041 Coral to Amber, E fr Trenton av to Blair, & S E fr Sepviva to 2018 Tulip, S W of Susq'ana av

DREXEL RD (W P), S W & S fr City av to N 58th

DROVE YARD LA (W P), W fr N 44th, bet Westminster av & Stiles

DRUMMOND'S PL, E fr 1749 Gtn av

DRURY, W fr 104 S 13th to S Juniper.

DRYDEN PL, S fr 228 Thompson

DUANE PL, N fr 1219 Ogden

DUDLEY, W fr S Water to 1027 S 2d & fr S 4th to S 10th, S of Hoffman

DUDLEY PL, S fr 514 Christian

DUNCAN (Bln), E fr Pennypack to Bln pike, & fr Murray to Lott, N of Banes

DUNCAN (Fkd), S E fr Tacony to Frankford creek, N E of Church

SHEET ASPHALT PAVING of all kinds.

DUNCANNON (Gtn), E fr Wister to Bustleton pike, S of Fisher's la & (Olney), W fr Clinton, S of Tabor av

DUNGAN'S AV, W fr 1070 Gtn av to N 2d

DUNK'S FERRY RD (Byberry), E fr Gravel rd to Bucks County line, S of Mechanicsville rd

DUNN'S CT, E fr 759 S 6th to Fulton

DUNTON, N fr 19 Wildey to Girard av

DUPONT (Myk), N W fr High to Mitchell & N E fr Ridge av to Magdalena, S E of Leverington av

DURFOR, W fr S 2d to S 5th, & fr 2112 S 11th to 2113 S 13th, bel Wolf

DURHAM (Gtn), S W fr 7130 Gtn av to Cresheim rd, N W of Mt Pleasant (See also E Durham)

DUROSS CT, W fr 784 S 6th

DUROSS PL, E fr 861 N 13th

DUTTON'S CT, S fr 620 Wash'n av

DUVAL (Gtn), S W fr Gtn av to Chew, ab Wash'n la (See also E Duval)

DYRE (Fkd), E fr Penn to Charles, bel Bridge

E.

E, N fr 2900 Ktn av & Cambria W of F to Cheltenham av

EADOM, N E fr Haworth to Sanger & fr Cottman to Bleigh, N W of Tacony

EAGLE, E fr 1051 Leopard

EAGLE AV, W fr 1220 N Front to Hope

EAGLEFIELD PL (W P), N fr 4031 Cambridge

EARL, S E fr Belgrade to 425 E Thompson & fr E Girard av to Richmond, W of Palmer

EARLHAM (Gtn), S W fr Cumberland, N W of Coulter

EARLHAM TER (Gtn), E fr Morris to Tacoma, S of School

EARP, W fr S Howard to S Hancock, S 2d to S American, Moyam'g av to S 9th, 1334 S 18th to S 19th & fr S 21st to S 23d, S of Wharton

EAST, S fr Wiccacoe av to Government av, E of Beaver

EAST (Myk), N E fr Cresson to Dexter, N W of Seville

E ALLEGHENY AV, E fr 3201 N Front to Del riv

E ALLEN, E fr 1035 N Front to E Palmer, & Bdg, fr Clapier to Jenks

E ARIZONA, E fr Jasper to 2320 Trenton av, S of E York

E ATLANTIC, E fr F, N W fr 3538 Fkd av to E Venango & fr Gaul to Belgrade, N of Tioga

E AUBURN, E fr Ormes to B, 2829 Arbor to D, Fkd av to Cedar & fr Gaul to 2840 Salmon, S of William

E BIRCH, N W fr 2938 Salmon to Belgrade & E fr 2930 Fkd av to Amber

E BOSTON, S E fr Ktn av to Amber, Trenton av to E Thompson & fr Edgemont to Salmon, E of E York

E BUTLER, E fr N Front to Del riv, N of E Erie av

E CABOT, N E fr Marlborough to 1246 E Oxford, 1243 E Palmer to E Montg'y av & fr 2469 E Dauphin to E York, E of E Thompson

E CAMBRIA, E fr 2901 N Front to Cedar

E CHELTEN AV (Gtn), E fr 5701 Gtn av to Stenton av

E CLAPIER (Gtn), E fr Gtn av to Baynton, S of Wister

E CLEARFIELD, E fr 3101 N Front to Del riv

E CLEMENTINE, E fr Ktn av to Trenton av & fr Richmond to Cedar, N of E Clearfield

E CLIVEDEN (Gtn), N E fr 6445 Gtn av to Chew, N of Johnson

E COLUMBIA AV, S E fr 1623 Fkd av to Del riv, S W of Palmer

E COMMISSIONER, E fr Gaul to Belgrade, & fr Martha to Collins, N of Indiana

E CORNWALL, E fr 3319 Ktn av to Emerald, N of E Westmoreland

E COULTER (Gtn), E fr 5401 Gtn av to Hancock

E CUMBERLAND, E fr 2501 N Front to Ktn av, thence S E to Del riv

E DAKOTA, E fr 2309 Amber to Trenton av, fr 2307 Tulip & fr Belgrade to Almond, E of E York

E DAUPHIN, S E fr 2243 N Front to Moyer

E DURHAM (Mt Airy), E fr Chew to Boyer, N E of Mt Pleasant av

RICHARDSON & ROSS, 30th & Race Sts.

E DUVAL (Gtn), N E fr Gtn av to Chew, S of E Johnson

E ELKHART, S E 'r Boudinot to D, Malvern to Fkd av. Helen to Wyoming, Joyce to Braddock, Gaul to Salmon & fr Richmond to Del riv, S of E Clearfield

E ERIE AV, E fr 3701 N Front to Del riv

E ESTAUGH, W fr Palethorp to N Howard, N of Ontario

E EVERGREEN AV (O Hill), S E fr 8601 Gtn av to County line rd, N E of Highland av

E EYRE, N E fr 1757 Fkd av to Memphis, S fr E Thompson & N E fr Girard av to Robinson

E FIRTH, S E fr 2507 Jasper to Amber, & fr Collins to Almond, N of E Cumberland

E FLETCHER, S fr Emerald to Amber, S of E Dauphin, S E fr Sepviva to Cedar, N of E Susquehanna av, 819 E Belgrade to Gaul & S E fr Mercer to 825 Richmond

E GARFIELD (Gtn), N E fr 5009 Gtn av to Wakefield, N W of E Seymour

E GEORGE, N E fr E Columbia av, N E of Wildey

E GIRARD AV, E fr 1201 Fkd av to E Norris

E GORDON, W fr Almond to Collins, S of E York

E HAINES (Gtn), E fr 5901 Gtn av to Old York rd

E HAROLD, S E fr 2619 Ktn av to Emerald, 2607 Martha to Moyer & fr Almond to 2610 E Thompson

E HARPER, E fr E Susq'ana av to E Fletcher, S E of E Girard av

E HARTWELL AV (O Hill), E fr 8201 Gtn av to Stenton av

E HAZZARD, S E fr 2553 Ktn av to Coral, & fr Collins to Moyer, S of E Huntingdon

E HEWSON, E fr E Girard av to Wildey, E Thompson to Sepviva, Blair to Trenton av, S of E Norris & fr E Belgrade to Salmon, S of E Somerset

E HILTON, E fr F to Sundgard & fr Ktn av to Jasper, N of E Allegheny av

E HORTTER (Gtn), N E fr Gtn av to Chew, at Pennypack

E HUNTINGDON, E fr 2601 N Front, to Del riv

E INDIANA, E fr 3000 N Front to Del riv

E JOHNSON (Gtn), E fr 6401 Gtn av to Stenton av

E JUNIATA (N Town), E fr Gtn av to Old York rd, & fr N 11th to Powder Mill rd

E KERBAUGH, N W fr 3972 Richmond

E LEHIGH AV, E fr 2701 N Front to B, thence S E to Richmond

E LETTERLY, S E fr 2457 Ktn av to Amber, & E fr 2451 Fkd av to Moyer, S of E Cumberland

E LIPPINCOTT, E fr A to Emerald, N of Clementine, Amber to Trenton av & fr Richmond to Del riv, S of E Allegheny av

E LOGAN (Gtn), E fr 4841 Gtn av to Fisher's la, ab Loudon

E LUZERNE, E fr 4001 N Front to Ktn av, thence E to Del riv, S of Roxb

E MADISON, E fr G to Sundgard, Ktn av to 3220 Fkd av, & fr Cedar to Allen, N of E Allegheny av

E MAYFIELD, N fr Edgemont to E Thompson, S of Judge

E MERMAID AV (O. Hill), E fr 7701 Gtn av to Stenton av, S of E Moreland av

E MONMOUTH, E fr 2927 Ktn av to Trenton av, Gaul to Salmon, N E of William & S E fr 2921 Melvale to Bath

E MONTGOMERY AV, E fr 1801 N Front to Richmond

E MORELAND AV (O Hill), E fr 7801 Gtn av to County line rd, N of E Mermaid av

E MOUNT AIRY AV (Mt A), E fr 7201 Gtn av to Cheltenham av

E MOUNT PLEASANT AV (Mt A), E fr 7101 Gtn av to Cheltenham av

E NASSAU, W fr Memphis to Tulip, W of E Somerset

E NICETOWN LA (N Town), N E fr N Front, to Ktn av, N of Pike

E NORRIS, E fr 1957 N Front to Del riv

E OAKDALE, E fr 2651 Ktn av to 2991 Fkd av, thence to Del riv

E ONTARIO, S E fr 3401 N Front to Del riv

E ORLEANS, E fr Ktn av to 2958 Fkd av, & E fr 2955 Fkd av to Amber

ASPHALTUM BLOCKS and TILES.

E OXFORD, S E fr Fkd av to
Wildey, N of Marlborough

E PACIFIC, E fr Ktn av to Jasper,
& fr Richmond to Allen, N of
E Venango

E PALMER, E fr N Front to Beach,
S of E Montg'y av

E PENN (Gtn), E fr 5321 Gtn av to
Chew & Stenton av

E PHIL ELLENA (Gtn), E fr Gtn
av to Chew, N of Hortter

E RITTENHOUSE (Gtn), E fr Gtn
av to Underhill, S of Haines

E RUSH, S E fr 2817 Fkd av to
Tulip, N of E Somerset

E RUSSELL, E fr Ktn av to N
Del av, N of Ontario

E SCHILLER, E fr G, Ktn av to
Fkd av, 3407 Richmond to Del riv,
S of Tioga

E SCHOOL (Gtn), E fr Gtn av ab
Church la

E SEDGWICK (Gtn), N E fr 7023
Gtn av to Stenton av, N of Gorgas

E SELTZER, E fr 2743 N Front to
A, Jasper to Helen, S E fr Coral
to Tulip, S of E Somerset, & fr
Belgrade to Salmon, N of E Lehigh av

E SERGEANT, S E fr 2535 Ktn av
to Almond, & fr 2535 E Thompson
to Richmond

E SEYMOUR (Gtn), N E fr 4951
Gtn av to Wakefield

E SHARPNACK (Gtn), N E fr 6601
Gtn av to Cheltenham av, N of
Upsal

E SILVER, E fr N Front to A,
S E fr Jasper to Helen, Emerald
to 2746 Fkd av & fr 2741 Coral
to Martha, N E of E Lehigh av

E SOMERSET, E fr 2755 N Front
to Ktn av, thence S E to Richmond

E SOUTHAMPTON AV (C Hill), E
fr 8301 Gtn av to Stenton av, S
of E Union av

E SPRINGFIELD AV (C Hill), E
fr 7901 Gtn av to County line rd,
N of E Moreland av

E STAFFORD (Gtn), E fr S W of
Lena to Baynton, N W of Chelten av

E STELLA, W fr 3022 Fkd av to
Elkhart, & E fr 2979 Fkd av to
Amber

E STERNER, E fr N Front to A,
S E fr Jasper to Helen, & N W
fr 2734 Fkd av to Emerald, & fr
Aramingo av to Miller, N of E
Lehigh av

E SUSQUEHANNA AV, E fr 2201
N Front to Del riv

E THAYER, E fr G, S of Ontario
& fr 3353 Ktn av

E THOMPSON, E & S fr 1301 Fkd
av to Hagert, & N E fr 2629 E
Somerset to Bdg

E TIOGA, E fr 3501 N Front to
Del riv

E TORONTO, S E fr 2983 E Thompson to Edgemont & fr 2965 Melvale to Del riv, N of Oakdale

E TUCKER, S E fr 2629 Martha
to Cedar, S W of Lehigh av

E TULPEHOCKEN (Gtn), E fr 6201
Gtn av to Limekiln turnpike

E UNION AV (O Hill), E fr 8401
Gtn av to Stenton av, S of Sharpnack

E UPSAL (Gtn), E fr 6501 Gtn av

E VENANGO, S E fr 3600 N Front
to Del riv, N of Tioga

E VICTORIA, W fr Balfour to
Richmond, N of E Venango

E WALNUT LA (Gtn), E fr 6101
Gtn av to Cheltenham av

E WALTER, N E fr 1207 E Co-
lumbia av to E Palmer, N of E
Girard av, 1217 E Montg'y av to
Berks, & W fr Burleigh, N W of
E Girard av

E WASHINGTON LA (Gtn), E fr
6301 Gtn av to Stenton av, ab
Tulpehocken

E WENSLEY, E fr 3335 Ktn av to
Emerald, & N fr Richmond to Del
riv, N of E Westmoreland

E WESTMORELAND, E fr 3301
Fkd av to Del riv

E WILDEY, N E fr 1055 Fkd av
to E Fletcher, N W of Richmond

E WILLARD, E fr G to Sundgard,
Ktn av to Emerald & fr Jasper to
Aramingo av, N of E Allegheny
av

E WILLIAM, S E fr B to Ormes,
2849 Fkd av to Tulip & Cedar to
Del riv, & (Bdg) S fr Pratt to Ash
S of Bridge

E WILLOW GROVE AV (C Hill),
E fr 8001 Gtn av to Stenton av,
N of Springfield av

RICHARDSON & ROSS, 30th & Race Sts.

CLAIMS AND LITIGATED MATTERS.

E WILT, N E fr Tulip to beyond Belgrade, N of E Montg'y av, E Girard av to 623 Wildey, & fr 1019 E Columbia av

E WISHART, E fr 3159 Ktn av to 3144 Fkd av, 3163 Amber to Trenton av & S E fr 3151 Richmond to Bath, S of E Allegheny av

E YORK, S E fr 2303 N Front to Beach

EASTBURN AV (Pittville), N E fr Stenton av to Limekiln turnpike, ab N 66th

EASTWICK AV, S fr 1606 Ogden

EASTWICK AV (W P), W fr S 45th to S 85th to S of Gibson av

EATON PL, S fr 24 Wildey to Eagle

EDEN PL, S fr 228 Catharine

EDGAR, W fr S 18th to Penrose av, N of Wolf

EDGAR PL, S fr 926 Pine

EDGELEY, W fr N Reese to N Fairhill, Delhi to 2133 N 10th, 2110 N 15th to N 18th & fr N 29th to N 30th, N of Diamond

EDGEMONT, N fr 2701 E York to Ash & (Bdg) fr Kirkbride to Pratt, W of Richmond

EDGEWOOD (W P) (See N & S Edgewood)

EDISON AV (Somerton)

EDMUND (Fkd), N fr Orthodox to Vankirk, ab Trenton R R. & (Tacony) fr Comly to Township line rd, W of Tulip

EDWARD, W fr 1156 N Hancock to N 2d

EDWIN, W fr 1720 Ridge av to 1845 Perkiomen

EISEN AV, W fr 1442 N 4th to N Lawrence

ELBERON AV (Fox Chase), S W fr Hoffnagle to Newtown & N Y R R, S E of Pine rd

ELBOW LA, W fr 22 Bank to S 3d

ELDER (R Sun), N fr Atlantic to Erie av, E of Gtn av

ELDRIDGE PL, E fr 1817 N 6th

ELEANOR (F'ville), E fr N 3d, N of Loudon

ELIZABETH (Fkd), N fr Church to Gillingham, N W of Leiper

ELIZABETH PL, E fr 1433 Hope

ELKHART, W fr N American to N 3d, S of Clearfield (See also E Elkhart)

ELLA, N fr E. Cambria to E Indiana & (Olney), N of Tabor rd, E of A

ELLEN, W fr 940 N Front to Mascher

ELLEN PL, E fr 751 S Front

ELLET (Gtn), N E fr McCallum, ab Sedgwick

ELLIS LA (Pville), N fr Woodland av, W of S 61st

ELLSWORTH, W fr S Swanson to S 3d, 1114 S 5th to S Randolph, and fr 1126 S 7th to Schuylkill av

ELLWOOD LA, W fr N 2d to 3125 Gtn av, N W of connecting R R

ELMWOOD AV (W P), S W fr Gibson av & S 56th to Island rd, S E of Gray's av

ELSER (N Town), N fr McFerran to Lycoming, E of Nice, W of N Broad

ELSINOR, N fr Roxb to Cayuga, W of J

ELWYN (Fkd), N fr Scattergood to Fraley, S of Trenton R R

ELY (Gtn), S fr 510 Haines to R R

EMERALD, N E fr 2201 N Front to E Lehigh av & N & S fr 2000 E Somerset, thence N to Erie av

EMERICK, W fr 439 Belgrade to Memphis, S of E Palmer

EMERSON (Fox Chase), S E fr D, S W of Hoffnagle

EMERY, N fr 1015 Shackamaxon to Day, fr E Columbia av W of Richmond, E Cumberland to E Luzerne & (Bdg) fr 2743 Bucklus to Ash

EMILY, W fr S Water to Moyam'g av, S 4th to S 8th, S 9th to S Percy, S 10th to S 13th, & fr 2014 S 15th to S 16th, S of McKean

EMINENCE (Roxb), S E fr Hildeburn & N W fr Hampton to McFadden & fr Manatawna to Northwestern av

EMLEN (Gtn), N W fr Carpenter to Cresheim creek, S W of Quincy

ENGLISH ROW (Myk), W fr Roxborough to Cotton, ab Cresson

ERDMAN, N E fr 821 Perkiomen

ERDMANN'S AV, W fr 830 N 15th

ERDRICK (Tacony), N E fr Sanger to Longshore, N E of Bristol & (Hbg) N E fr Decatur to Bustleton R R

ERIE AV, W fr 3700 N Front to Hunting Park av, N of Venango (See also E Erie av)

ERNST, W fr 2516 S 28th

ERWIG AV (Pville), S W fr S 85th, E of Laycock av

SHEET ASPHALT PAVING of all kinds.

ESHER'S AV, N fr 1209 Fairmount av

ESHNER PL, E fr 1007 N Orianna

ESTAUGH, W fr N Howard to Palethorp, & W fr N 17th to N 23d, N of Ontario

ETTING, N fr Walter to Stiles, Master to Jefferson, Montg'y av to Glenwood av, & fr Sedgley av to Page, W of N 27th

EUCLID, W fr 10th to N Warnock, N Broad to N 15th, & fr N 30th to N 32d. S of Berks

EUGENE AV, E fr 225 S Sydenham

EVA (Roxb), N W fr Dearnley to Streeper, N E of Silverwood

EVANS, N fr 2111 E Elkhart to E Clearfield, W of Trenton av

EVANS (Bln), E fr Pennypack to Lott, N of Starkey

EVANS AV, E fr 1071 Gtn av

EVELINE (Falls), E fr Frederick, S of Stanton

EVERGREEN (Myk), S fr Rex, N E of Ridge av

EVERGREEN AV (C Hill), S W fr 8600 Gtn av to Wiss av, N W of Highland av (See also E Evergreen av)

EWALD PL, N fr 1811 Naudain

EWELL PL, S fr 2724 Eyre

EWING'S PL, W fr 712 S American

EXETER (Roxb), E fr Pechin, bel Roxb

EYRE, W fr 1740 N 27th to N 28th, & fr N 31st to Natrona, S of Montg'y av (See also E Eyre)

F.

F, N fr 3000 Ktn av, & E Indiana to Cheltenham av, E of E

FACTORY (Fkd), N E fr Adams, N of Church

FAGEN'S PL, S fr 1714 Lombard

FAIRBANK PL, E fr S American, S of Locust

FAIRFAX AV (Gtn), N fr Price, W of Evans

FAIRHILL (Oak Lane), S fr 66th av to 65th av, E of N 6th. (See also N & S Fairhill)

FAIRHILL PARK, W fr N 4th to N 5th & fr Huntingdon to Lehigh av

FAIRMOUNT AV, W fr 700 N Del av to Fairmount Park & (W P) fr N 32d to N 50th, S of Aspen

FAIRMOUNT PARK, N fr N 25th to Penna av, to N 33d, to Ridge av, to Wissahickon & C Hill. N W fr Spg Garden to Girard av, to Parkside av, to Gorgas la, to Crestline av, to Schuyl riv

FAIRTHORNE AV (Roxb), E fr Ridge av, N of Gorgas la

FAIRVIEW (Hbg), N E of Welsh rd, N W of Crispin

FALLON (W P) (See N & S Fallon)

FALLS PL, N fr 539 Race

FALLS RD (Falls), N W fr N Broad to Falls of Schuyl

FARINA (Fkd), S E fr Penn to Franklin, S W of Sellers

FARMVILLE, N fr Girard av, W of N 68th

FARSON, (See N & S Farson)

FAWN (See N & S Fawn)

FEDERAL, W fr 1200 S Front to Gray's Ferry rd & (W P) fr Baltimore av to Del county line

FEINOUR'S PL, S fr r of 736 Swanson

FELTON (See N & S Felton)

FELTON PL, N fr 131 Fitzwater

FERDINAND (Pittville), N W fr Wash'n la to Johnson, N E of Mansfield

FERN PL, N fr 1319 Cambridge

FERNBERGER AV, W fr 1336 N Lawrence to N 5th

FERNON, W fr 1622 S Front to 1603 Moyam'g av, S 5th to S 7th, S 8th to S 11th & fr S 17th to S 23d, S of Tasker

FERRY (Falls), W fr 4100 Ridge av

FERRY (Roxb), W fr Ridge av, N of Manatawna rd

FERRY LA (Hbg), E fr Bristol rd N of Pennypack la

FIELDS, N fr 1629 Francis

FIFE'S PL, S fr 1424 Kater to Bainbridge

FILBERT, W fr N Del av to N Front, fr 23 N 2d, W fr 40 N 2d to W of N 3d & fr 36 N 6th to Schuyl riv, & (W P) W fr N 33d to N 41st & fr N 42d, N of Market

FILLMORE (See A)

FILLMORE (Bdg), N W fr E Thompson to Almond, N E of Buckius

FILLMORE (Fkd), S E fr Fkd av to Willow, N W fr Horrocks to P & S E fr Hawthorne to Edmund, N of Foulkrod

RICHARDSON & ROSS, 30th & Race Sts.

EQUITABLE RATES—PROMPT RETURNS.

FILLMORE AV, W fr 126 N 15th
FIRTH, W fr N 8th to N 9th, 2512
N 12th to N 13th, N 15th to
N Sydenham, N 22d to N 26th, &
N 33d to N 34th. N of Cumberland
(See also E Firth)
FISHER'S LA (Gtn), E fr E Logan
to Frankford, S of Duncannon
FISHER'S PL, W fr 1326 Gtn av
to N Orianna
FISK AV (Falls), E fr Cresson, N
of Calumet
FITZGERALD, W fr 2326 S 4th to
S 5th & fr S 11th to S 13th, S
of Wolf
FITZWATER, W fr 748 S Del av
to Gray's Ferry av & (W P) S W
fr S 59th to S 64th
FLATROCK AV (Myk), N fr Colum-
bia bridge, W of the Canal
FLEMING (Myk), S E fr Roxb to
Hermitage, Lyceum to Lever-
ington av, N E of Terrace
FLEMING (W P), W fr N 52d to
N 53d, N of Market
FLEMING'S LA, S E fr League
Island rd, n Av 39 S, to Schuy'l
FLETCHER, W fr Sedgely av to
N 31st, N of Susq'ana av
(See also E Fletcher)
FLICKWIR CT, N fr 227 Fitzwater
FLOOD'S PL, W fr 908 S 6th
FLORENCE AV (W P), S W fr
Baltimore av & S 48th to Cobb's
creek, N W of Amaseka
FLORIST, W fr 216 N Front to W
of N 2d, N 3d to N 4th, 224 N
13th to N Juniper, & fr N Mole to
N Hicks, N of Race
FOLSOM, W fr 716 N 17th to N
18th 764 N 26th to Taney, N
27th to Pennock, & (W P) fr N
38th to Union, & fr N 48th to N
50th, N of Fairmount av
FONTAIN, W fr 2012 N Howard to
Mascher, 2030 N 15th to N 20th,
fr N Croskey to N 23d, & fr N
30th to N 32d, S of Diamond
FORD RD (W P), E fr Belmont av
to Schuy'l riv bel Conshohocken av
FOREST AV (Gtn), W fr Wash'n
av to Sharpnack, S of William
FORREST PL, E fr 621 S American
FOTTERALL SQ (28th ward), N
11th to N 12th, York to Cumberland
FOULKROD (Fkd), S E fr Castor
to Glenloch, S W of Harrison

FOUNTAIN (Myk & Roxb), N E fr
Main to Magdalena, N of Her-
mitage
FOUST (Fkd), E fr Bristol pike
to Del riv, S of Van Kirk
FOWLER (Myk), N W fr Greenough
to Ripka, & fr 248 Hermitage
to Fountain av
FOX (N Town), N fr Allegheny av
to Mill, E of McMichael
FOX CHASE RD (Bln), N W fr
Bustleton pike to Meeting House
rd, W of Axe Factory rd
FOX SQ, S E fr Gaul to Belgrade,
N E fr Tioga to Atlantic
FOX'S CT, S fr 1224 Fitzwater
FRACKER (Gtn), W fr Cheltenham
& Willow Grove pike, S of Chel-
tenham av
FRALEY (Fkd), W fr Tacony, ab
Kennedy
FRANCIS, S W fr 1620 Ridge av
to Shirley
FRANCONI PL, E fr 715 N 9th
FRANK (Gtn), N E fr Wiss av to
Lincoln av, S E of Carpenter
FRANKFORD (Fkd), N W fr Fkd
Creek to Wakeling, N E of Tucker
FRANKFORD AV, N E fr Laurel,
ab Beach, to Fkd creek, thence
through Fkd to Bristol turnpike,
E of Franklin
FRANKFORD AV (Hbg), fr Forrest
Home N E to Pennypack creek
FRANKLIN (See N & S Franklin)
FRANKLIN (Fkd), N fr Pine to
Wakeling, W of Fkd av
FRANKLIN (Gtn), N fr Oak la to
Montg'y county line, E of N P R R
FRANKLIN SQ, N fr Race to Vine,
& W fr N 6th to N Franklin
FRAZIER (W P). (See N & S Fra-
zier)
FREDERICK (Falls), S fr 125 Stan-
ton, N of Ridge av
FREEDLEY, E fr 2509 Cedar to
Gaul, N of E Cumberland
FREELAND AV (Wiss), N W fr
Wiss to Sumac, N E of Myk av, &
(Roxb), S fr Levering to Ritten-
house, E of Pechin
FREESTON'S PL, E fr 1007 Moy-
am'g av
FRENCH, W fr. N Hutchinson to
2135 N 10th, N 13th to Park av,
N 15th to N 18th, Marston to N
27th, & fr N 29th to N 32d, S of
Susq'ana av

ASPHALTUM BLOCKS and TILES.

FRIENDSHIP (Tacony), N fr Wissinoming to Trenton R R & fr Keystone to Ditman, E of Princeton.
FRIENDSHIP PL, E fr 627 N American
FRITSCH, W fr K, N of Tioga
FROGMOOR (Fkd), E fr Powdermill la, along S side Fkd creek
FROMBERGER'S CT, W fr 322 N American
FRONT (See N & S Front)
FULLER (Hbg), S W fr Crispin to Ryan, & fr Fkd av to Del riv, N of Pennypack la
FILMER (Bln), S E fr Meeting House rd to Starkey, ab Lott
FULMORE (Bln), E fr Pennypack to Bustleton rd, N of Bln pike
FULTON, W fr 782 S 2d to S 3d, E f: 767 & W fr 770 S 4th to S 5th, S Randolph to S 6th, E from 771 S 7th & W fr S 7th to S 8th, S Juniper to S Clarion, S 20th to S 24th, &E fr S Taney, N of Catharine
FULTON CT, W fr 1417 Hewson
FURLONG CT, N fr 707 Cherry

G.

G, N fr Ktn av & E Clearfield to Strahle, E of F
GAINES PL, N fr 229 Queen
GALLOWAY, N fr 307 Green to 318 Brown, & fr 307 George to Allen
GARDEN (Bdg), N fr Jenks to Fkd creek
GARFIELD (Gtn), N W fr Seymour to Manheim, N E of Greene (See also E Garfield)
GARNET (See N & S Garnet)
GARRETSON PL, E fr 837 S 3d
GARVIN PL, S fr 236 Catharine
GASKILL, W fr 518 S 2d to S 5th
GATES (Myk), N E fr P & R Rw to Umbria, 4169 Main to Mitchell, & fr Mansion to Fowler, S W of Fountain & (Roxb) N E fr Wood
GATZMER, W fr 120 S Del av to S Water, & fr S Front to S 2d, S of Chestnut
GAUL, N fr E Montg'y av to Fkd creek, E of Cedar
GAY (Myk), N W fr Main to Fleming, N W of Levering
GAY CT, W fr 1230 N 3d
GEARY, W fr Del riv to Schuy'l riv, 3300 S

GEBHART CT, S fr 1626 Carlton
GENOESE PL, S fr 328 Master
GENTLEMEN'S DRIVING PARK, Crestline av, N W boundary line of Fairmount Park, N of Belmont
GEORGE, W fr 1046 N 2d to N 5th, 912 N 13th, 90S N 19th to N 21st, & fr N 27th to N 28th, N of Poplar (See also E George)
GEORGE'S AV (W P), S W of Crestline av, boundary av of W Park
GERHARD (Roxb), N fr Ridge av to Houghton, N W fr Roxb
GERMANTOWN AV, N W fr N Front & Laurel to township line
GERRITT, W fr 1330 S Howard to S Hancock, Moyam'g av to S Philip, S 3d to S Lawrence, S 5th to S 7th, Dickinson to S 12th, 1410 S 12th to S 13th, S 18th to S 21st & fr S 22d to S 23d, S of Reed
GETTYSBURG AV (Roxb), N fr Isabella to Port Royal av, S W of Ridge av
GETZELL PL, N fr 1219 Poplar
GIBSON AV, S W fr S 52d to Bow creek, N W of P & R R W
GIBSON'S CT, E fr 817 N Orianna
GIBSON'S PT, fr Schuy'l riv to S 58th
GIDEON, N fr 809 Wood
GIHON PL, W fr 1222 Carlisle
GILLESPIE (Fkd), N E fr Bridge to Pearson, N W of Jackson and Tacony, N E fr Longshore to Cottman, N W of Gregg
GILLINGHAM (Fkd), N W fr Worth to Hedge, N E of Oxford & fr Fkd av to Oakland, N E of Sellers
GILMORE PL, E fr 926 N American
GILPIN PL, W fr 842 N Lawrence to N Orkney
GINNODO, W fr 1820 Ridge av to N 19th, N of Poplar
GIRARD, W fr S 11th to S 12th, S of Market
GIRARD AV, W fr 1200 Fkd av to Girard College, & fr N Stillman to Bridge at Schuy'l riv, thence to N 69th (See also E Girard av)
GIRARD PARK (26th ward), S 20th to S 23d, Porter, Oregon & Penrose av
GLAZIER PL, E fr 917 N 3d
GLENAT'S AV, N fr 33 Poplar

RICHARDSON & ROSS, 30th & Race Sts.

GLENLOCH (Fkd), E fr Tucker to Bridge, N of Ditman & (Tacony) N E fr Longshore to Cottman, N W of Ditman

GLENMORE (P'ville), S W fr S 48th to Hanson, fr Hay la to S 65th, & fr S 68th to Island rd, S E of Paschall av, & fr S 73d, S of R R

GLENVILLE PL, W fr 828 N 15th

GLENWOOD AV, S W fr 3600 N Front & Venango to N 33d & Master, S W of R R

GODDARD PL, E fr 1311 S 10th

GODFREY (Gtn), W fr N 20th to Stenton av, N of Church la

GOLDBECK'S AV, E fr 1131 N 2d

GOLDSMITH'S CT, W fr 518 Mascher

GOODBREAD PL, S fr 1006 Reno

GOODMAN (N Town), S E fr Rising Sun la to Ellwood la, S of Ontario

GOODWIN PL, W fr 1454 Beach

GORDON, W fr Sedgley to Natrona, N of Dauphin (See also E Gordon)

GORDON PL, N fr 1831 Naudain

GORGAS (Gtn), N E fr 6901 Gtn av to Stenton av

GORGAS LA (Roxb), E fr Ridge av to Wiss creek, N of Hermitage

GORGAS PARK (21st ward), Ridge av to Myk av, Hermitage to W. of Gates

GOVERNMENT AV, fronting back channel, W fr Del av to Schuy'l riv

GOWEN AV (Gtn), E fr 7401 Gtn av to city line, N W of Mt Airy av

GRAMMANT PL, N fr 829 Carpenter

GRAMPIAN PL, E fr 705 N 13th

GRANGE (Gtn), W fr Beechwood to Stenton av, & (Olney), fr R to Van Kirk to N 20th, N of Chew

GRANITE, W fr 212 S Front to Dock

GRANITE (Fkd), S E fr Fkd av to Willow, Cottage to Jackson, Foulkrod to James, S of Melrose, N W of Bridge, & fr Leiper to T.

GRANSBACK, N fr E Cambria to E Clearfield, E of D

GRANT (Pittville)

GRANT AV (Torresdale), S E fr P R R to Poquessing av

GRANT'S CT, E fr 1413 N Alder

GRAPE (Myk), N E fr 4341 Main to Myk av

GRATZ, N fr Jefferson to Susqu'ana av, Dauphin to Huntingdon, & fr Cambria to Indiana, W of N 18th

GRAUCH PL, W fr 2320 N Marshall

GRAVEL HOLE LA, N W fr Old 2d, n Stone House la to S 5th

GRAVEL RD (Byberry), S E fr Bensalem pike to Poquessing cr'k

GRAVEL'S CT, S fr 1304 Olive

GRAVER'S LA (Gtn), N E fr N 30th to Stenton av, S E of Highland av

GRAY'S AV (Pville), S W fr S 48th to S 50th, S 62d to S 64th, & fr S 70th to S 73d, W of Elmwood av

GRAY'S FERRY AV, S W fr S 23d & South to Schuy'l riv, & W P

GRAY'S LA (W P), S fr Market to Elmwood av, W of S 55th (Gray's la N, now Redfield)

GREEN, W fr 600 N Del av to Fairmount pk

GREEN HILL PL, N fr 1635 Ogden

GREEN LA (Gtn), E fr Old York rd to Crescentville, S of Godfrey av

GREEN LA (Myk & Roxb), N E fr 4501 Main to Ridge av; S E of Dupont

GREENE (Gtn), N W fr G & N R R to Carpenter, S W of Gtn av

GREENOUGH (Myk), N E fr Mansion av to Wilde, N W of Leverington av

GREENVILLE, S W fr Wiccacoe av to Swanson, N of Porter

GREENVILLE PL, W fr 224 S. Sydenham

GREENWAY AV (W P), W fr S 47th to Cobb's creek, N of Woodland av

GREENWICH, W fr S Water to S 6th, S Marshall to 1515 S 7th, S 8th to Passy'k av, N W fr 1522 Passy'k av to Dickinson & fr S 22d to S 24th, S of Dickinson

GREENWOOD PL, E fr 615 N Front

GREENWOOD PL, N fr 509 Noble

GREEVE'S AV (Gtn), S E fr Locust av, N E of Morton

GREGG (Bln), S E fr Meeting House rd to Starkey & fr Old Newtown rd to Bln & Somerton turnpike, ab Hermitage

SHEET ASPHALT PAVING of all kinds.

GRETNA TER (Falls), N fr Bowman, W of N 35th
GRIFFITH, S E fr 810 E Thompson to Moyer, S W of Fletcher
GRIM'S AV, W fr 912 N 3d
GROSS (W P), N fr Arch to Media & fr Woodbine av to Jefferson, W of N 63d
GROVE, S fr 3528 Wharton to Reed & (W P) S fr 3467 Sansom
GROVER'S AV (Torresdale)
GUARDIAN AV (W P), S W fr Pine ab S 34th, between University & Almshouse
GUENTHER, S fr Oakford to Reed, W of S 28th
GUEST, W fr Hope to 1611 N Howard & fr N 32d to Natrona, N of Oxford
GUILFORD PL, E fr 619 S American
GURNEY, S E fr E Somerset to S W of Reading Rw
GYPSY LA (Wiss), N W fr School House la to Wiss av, ab Reading R R

H.

H, N fr Ktn av & E Allegheny av to Strahle, E of G, & (Lawndale)
HACKER PL, W fr 940 S 4th
HACKETT'S CT, S fr 438 Monroe
HADDINGTON (W P), S W fr N 56th to N 70th, N of Lansdowne av
HADFIELD (W P), S W fr 738 S 51st to S 52d
HAGERT, W fr N 13th to N Clarion, & fr 2423 N Carlisle to N 15th
HAGY (Roxb), fr Port Royal av to county line, W of Ridge av
HAHN CT, N fr 1915 Cuthbert
HAINES (Gtn), N W fr 5926 Gtn av to Wayne (See also E Haines)
HAINES (P'ville)
HALCYON AV, S fr Juniata, E of Clarissa
HALL, W fr 934 Moyam'g av to S Bodine, 908 S Orianna, 934 S 5th, E fr 923 S 8th, W fr 926 S 9th, & fr S Jessup to S Sartain
HALLOWELL AV, S fr 706 Poplar
HAMEL'S CT, S fr 1708 Lombard
HAMILTON, W fr 468 N 5th, 442 N Percy to N 25th, & (W P) fr N 31st to Lancaster av, ab Baring

HAMILTON'S CT, W fr 1328 N Front to N Hope
HAMMITT'S AV, N fr 1017 Crease, N W of Richmond
HANCOCK (See N & S Hancock)
HANCOCK'S CT, S fr 2126 Wood
HANOVER (See E Columbia av)
HANSBERRY (Gtn), N E fr Wiss av to Gtn av, ab Manheim
HANSON (W P), S fr Woodland av to Paschall av, E of S 49th
HARDING PL, S fr 322 Fitzwater
HARLAN, W fr 1416 N 4th to N Lawrence, & fr 1406 N 18th to N 27th, & (W P), E & W fr N 52d & W fr N 54th to Conestoga, N of Master
HARLEY (Pville), S W fr Gibson av & S 68th to Island rd, & fr S 79th to S 88th, N W of Eastwick av
HARLEY'S CT, N fr 2009 Market to Commerce
HARMAR, S fr S 33d to Schuyl av, S of Reed, Federal to Reed & B & O R R, W of S 35th
HARMER, W fr 866 N 11th to N 12th, & fr N Carlisle to W of N 16th S of Poplar
HARMONY (W P) (See N & S Harmony)
HARMONY CT, W fr 1504 Cadwallader to Gtn av
HARMONY CT, W fr 142 S 3d to S 4th
HARMSTEAD PL, S fr 912 Ogden
HAROLD, W fr N Wendle to N Marshall, 2614 N 12th to N 13th, & fr N 22d to N 27th, N of Huntingdon (See also E Harold)
HARPER, W fr 946 N 12th to N 13th, 918 N 17th to N 20th, N 27th to N 28th, N 29th to W of N 30th, S of Girard av (See also E Harper)
HARPER'S CT, S fr 2006 Lombard
HARPER'S CT, W fr 508 S 18th
HARPER'S PL, E fr 623 S American
HARRISON (Fkd), E fr Large to Jackson, N of Foulkrod
HARRISON'S CT (Gtn), N fr 1017 Pleasant
HARROWGATE PARK (25th ward), Ktn av, E Schiller & E Tioga
HART LA, N W fr 2822 Fkd av to E N Town la
HARTEL (Hbg), Del riv to Mont-g'y Co line, S W of Decatur

RICHARDSON & ROSS, 30th & Race Sts.

HARTLEY'S PL, S fr 1338 Cherry

HARTRANFT, W fr Del riv to Schuy'l, 3400 S

HARTSHORNE LA (Fkd), N E fr K of P Greenwood cem to Township line rd, E of Cedar Grove & Vol Town

HARTVILLE, N fr 541 E Cambria, W of E

HARTWELL AV (C Hill), W fr S200 Gtn av to Wiss pike, ab Abington av (See also E Hartwell av)

HARVEY (Gtn), W fr 6000 Gtn av to Wiss av

HARVEY (Myk), N E fr Cresson to Ridge av, Righter to Houghton & Rochelle av to Oros, S of Hermit

HARVEY'S CT, W fr 408 S 21st

HARVEY'S PL, E fr 1021 N American

HASKIN PL, S fr 220 Federal to Manton

HASSINGER AV, W fr 118 N Juniper

HATTERS PL, N fr 2315 Vine

HAVERFORD (W P), W fr N 30th to County line rd, N of Spg Garden

HAWORTH (Bdg), S E fr E Thompson, N E of Kirkbride (Fkd), N fr James to Glenloch, E of Fkd & N W fr Willow to Fkd av, N E of Wakeling

HAWTHORN AV, N fr 1701 Ludlow

HAWTHORNE (Fkd), S W fr Plum, & N E fr Meadow to Devereaux, N W of Mulberry

HAY LA (W P), S E fr Woodland av, ab S 62d

HAY'S CT, E fr 325 N American

HAYWOOD (Falls), S W fr Krail, bet Crawford & Indian Queen la

HAYWOOD PL, S fr 914 Hamilton

HAZEL AV (W P), W fr S 60th to S 63d, S of Lombard

HAZZARD, W fr N Philip to N American, 2536 N 12th to N 13th, N 15th to N Sydenham, & fr N 25th to N 26th, N of Cumberland

HECK PL, E fr 961 N 2d

HECK'S LA (Bln), E fr Bln pike

HEDGE (Fkd), N fr 101 E Unity to Meadow

HEDLEY (Bdg), E fr Richmond to Del riv, N of Juniata

HEFT'S CT (Myk), S E fr Cedar, S W of Cresson

HEGERMAN (Tacony), N E fr Sanger, S E of Torresdale av

HEISKELL (Gtn), N fr Baynton, W of Morton

HEISS PL, W fr 423 Moyer

HELEN, N fr 358 E Somerset to Clearfield, Ontario to a pt. W of Emerald, & fr E Tioga to E Venango, E of Jasper

HELLERMAN (Tacony), S E fr P R R to Del riv, S of Penn

HEMBERGER, N fr Berks to Norris, & fr Cambria to Indiana, E of N 23d

HEMLOCK TER (Wiss), N E fr Righter to Vicaris, ab Sumac

HENDERSON CT, S fr 1032 Rodman to South

HENRY (P'ville), S fr Catharine, W of S 62d

HENVIS (N Town), W fr Hunting Park av to Ruffner, E of Gtn av

HERBERT (Bdg), S E fr Belgrade to School, & (Fkd), N W fr Tacony creek to Mulberry & fr Horrocks to Castor rd, S of Foulkrod

HERBERT PL, N fr 1221 Commerce

HERITAGE (Bln), S E fr Meeting House rd to Starkey, ab Nestor

HERMAN (Gtn), E fr 6115 Gtn av to Morton

HERMIT (Wiss, Myk & Roxb), N E fr Cresson to Wiss av, N W of Harvey

HERMITAGE (Myk), E fr P & N R R to Smick, thence to Magdalena, W of Levering, S E of Wright

HESS (Hbg), fr Craig to Crispin

HESTON (W P), S E fr N 51st, N of Jefferson to P R R, W of Belmont av

HEWSON, W fr N Mascher to Waterloo, N 4th to N 5th, 1916 N 17th to N 18th, N 19th to N Uber & fr N 32d to N 33d, N of Berks (See also E Hewson)

HICKMAN'S CT, N fr 815 Willow

HICKORY (Hbg), E fr Erdrick to Holmesburg N of Mill

HICKORY CT, S fr 604 Willow

HICKS (See N & S Hicks)

HIGBEE (Wissinoming), N W fr Torr av to Walker, S E of Comly

HIGH (Gtn), E fr 5933 Gtn av to Chew, N W of Haines

HIGH (Myk), S E fr Umbria to Green la, N E of Main

ASPHALTUM BLOCKS and TILES.

HIGHLAND AV (C Hill), S W fr P G & C H R R to Wiss Creek, N W of Union
HIGHT'S AV, N fr 2509 Callowhill
HILDEBURN (C Hill), S W fr Sullivan to N 29th, N W of Norman
HILL'S CT, S fr 1824 Naudain
HILL'S LA (C Hill), S E fr Mermaid av, W of N 35th
HILL'S MILL RD (Gtn), W fr Cresheim to Wiss av, N of Allen's la
HILLES (Fkd), E fr Fkd av to Orchard, S of Womrath
HILLSIDE AV (C Hill), W fr Bechtel rd to N 32d, N of Cresheim av
HILLSPACH (Bln), N E fr Welsh to Fulmer, S of Evans
HILTON, W fr Gtn av to N 13th, N 15th to N Sydenham, & E fr N 20th, N of Allegheny av (See also E Hilton)
HOBENSACK PL, N fr 145 Fairmount av
HOFF (Bln), E fr Pennypack to Lott, N of Clark
HOFFMAN, E fr S Front to S Water & W fr 1912 S Front to S 2d, 1912 S 4th to S 8th & fr S 9th to 10th, S of Mifflin
HOFFMAN AV (W P), S W of S 54th & Baltimore av to Cobb's creek
HOFFNAGLE (Fox Chase), S E fr Montg'y Co line S W of Strahle
HOG ISLAND RD (W P), S fr Rope Ferry rd, W of Penrose Ferry Bridge
HOLLINGSWORTH, W fr N 31st to Natrora, N of Columbia av
HOLLY (W P) (See N & S Holly)
HOLLYWOOD, N fr Stiles to Oxford, W of N 29th & fr 2015 Columbia av to Glenwood av, & fr York to Cumberland
HOLMESBURG (Hbg), S W fr Fkd av to Ditman, parallel with Pennypack creek
HOLSTEIN AV (P'ville), S fr S 76th to S 90th, E of Erwig av
HOLT AV, W fr 620 Mascher
HOME PL, S fr 228 Fitzwater
HOMESTEAD (Wissino), S E fr State rd to Del river, N of Dark Run la
HOOPER (P'ville), W fr S 72d, N of Greenway av
HOOPES (W P), W fr 862 N 45th to N 50th, N of Parrish

HOPE, N fr 103 Pegg to Noble, 113 Nectarine to Fairmount av, 115 Poplar, 121 Laurel to Pollard, Allen to Erie av & fr Loudon to Rockland, W of N Front
HOPKINSON PL, W fr 124 N Juniper
HORN'S CT, E fr 825 Oriana
HORNER AV, E fr 247 N 13th
HORROCKS (Fkd), N E fr Unity to Olney av, W of Wingohocking
HORST'S CT, W fr 1730 Cadwallader
HORSTMAN'S CT, S fr 320 Fitzwater
HORSTMAN'S CT, S fr 940 Rodman
HORSTMANN'S ROW, E fr 777 S 3d
HORTTER (Gtn), S W fr 6600 Gtn av to Wiss av (See also E Hortter)
HOSPITAL LA (W P), N W fr Belmont av to N 49th, ab Midvale av.
HOUBEN'S PL, E fr 1147 N 3d
HOUDENS, W fr 252 N 15th
HOUGHTON (Roxb), S E fr Monastery av to Jamestown, N E of Ridge av
HOUSEKEEPER'S CT, W fr 1450 Beach
HOWARD (See N & S Howard)
HOWARD PL, S fr 1414 Brown
HOWARD TER (Mt A), N W fr Mt Airy av, n P & R R R
HOWELL (Tac), S E fr Fkd av to Del riv, N of Van Kirk
HOYT, W fr Del riv to Schuyl, 3500 S
HUGHES PL, W fr 1024 Moyam'g av
HULL PL, W fr 968 N Del av
HULSEMAN, W fr S 21st to S 25th, S of Curtin
HULSEMAN CT, S fr 1240 Fitzwater
HUMEL CT, E fr 943 N 3d
HUNTER'S LA (W P), S W fr Lancaster av, W of N 53d
HUNTING PARK (N Town), W fr N 9th to Old York rd, bet N Town la & Cayuga
HUNTING PARK AV (N Town), W fr N 15th & Juniata S of Bristol to Ridge av
HUNTINGDON, W fr 2600 N Front to N 21st & fr N 26th to Schuy'l riv (See also E Huntingdon)

RICHARDSON & ROSS, 30th & Race Sts.

HURLEY, S fr E Indiana to Hart la, W of D

HUSTON, S fr Wolf to Ritner, W of S 18th

HUTCHINSON, S fr Fisher's la, W of N 5th (See also N & S Hutchinson)

HUTTON (W P), N fr Wallace to Fairmount av & fr Parrish to Ogden, E of N 43d

I.

I, N fr Ktn av & E Westmoreland to Strahle, E of H & (Marburg)

IMOGENE (Fkd), N W fr Mercer to Leiper, N of Church & W fr Waln to Paul, S of Unity

INDEPENDENCE AV (Oak la), S fr Oak la, W of N 5th

INDEPENDENCE SQ, W fr S 5th to S 6th, S fr State House to Walnut

INDIAN QUEEN LA (Falls), E fr 4201 Ridge av to Wiss av, bet Abbotsford av & Stafford

INDIANA, W fr N Front to Schuy'l riv, 3000 N (See also E Indiana)

INGERSOLL, W fr 1326 N 15 to N Smedley, & fr Bidge av to N 18th, S of Master

INGRAM, W fr 1218 S 27th to S 28th

IONIC, W fr 112 S Front to S 3d, 114 S 7th to S 8th, 114 S 15th, 117 S 16th to S 18th, 110 S 20th, 106 S 23d to S 24th & (W P) W fr S 32d to S 33d & fr S 44th to S 45th, S of Chestnut

IOWA CT, S fr 208 De Lancey

IRENE PL, S fr 1202 Tasker

IRON PL, S fr 88 Laurel

IRVING, S 6th to S Franklin, 246 S Hutchinson to S Delhi, S Clifton to S Alder, S Jessup to S Marvine, 242 S 13th to S Juniper, & (W P), 32d to S 33d, S 37th to S 41st, S 50th to S 53d, & fr S 59th to S 60th, S of Locust

IRWIN'S CT, W fr 528 N 23d

ISABELLA (Gtn), N fr E Wash'n to Johnson, S W of Cemetery

ISABELLA (Roxb), W fr Ridge av, bel Shawmont av

ISEMINGER (See N & S Iseminger)

ISLAND RD (Pville), S fr Woodland av, W of S 73d

J.

J, N fr Ktn av & E Ontario to Strahle, E of I

JACKSON, W fr Del riv to Schuy'l riv, 2200 S

JACKSON (Fkd), N E fr Fillmore to Fitler, N W of Ditman

JACOB (Roxb), N E fr Myk av to Pechin, N W of Leverington av

JACOBY AV, N fr 187 Oxford

JAMES (Fkd), N E fr Orthodox to Van Kirk, ab Tacony

JAMES (Tacony), N E fr Princeton to Friendship, N W of Tacony

JAMES CT, W fr 1236 N Front

JAMESTOWN (Myk), N E fr 4141 Main to Myk av & fr Ridge av to Laros, ab Rittenhouse

JAMISON'S CT, N fr 2309 Hamilton

JANES PL, W fr 1102 N Front

JANNEY, N fr 2633 Tucker to Oakdale, E of Sepviva, 2233 Auburn to William, & fr Ann to Luzerne, W of Tulip

JASPER, N E fr intersection of 2301 N Front & E Dauphin to E Lehigh av, fr Tusculum to E Cambria & fr E Clearfield to E Erie av

JAYNE AL (W P), W fr 34 N 32d

JEFFERSON, W fr 1500 Fkd av to Glenwood av, & (W P) S W fr Columbia av ab N 42d to N 52d, fr Lancaster av & N 56th to N 70th, N of Oxford

JEFFERSON (Gtn), N W fr Wash'n to Hortter, W of Gtn av

JEFFERSON SQ, W fr S 3d to S 4th, S fr Wash'n av to Federal

JEFFREY PL, W fr 1108 N Front

JENKINS PL, N fr 1315 Quarry

JENKS (Bdg), S fr Richmond to Del riv, bel Kirkbride

JERUSALEM PL, S fr 1202 Pearl

JESSUP (See N & S Jessup)

JEWETT, N fr Huntingdon, W of N 19th

JOHN (Fkd), W fr 4226 Josephine bel Oxford

JOHN'S PL, N fr 2421 Callowhill to Hamilton

JOHNSON (Blue Bell Hill), S W fr Wiss av to Walnut la, S E of Cliveden

JOHNSON (Gtn), W fr 6400 Gtn av to Wiss av, N W of Wash'n la (See also E Johnson)

SHEET ASPHALT PAVING of all kinds.

JOHNSTON, W fr Del riv to Schuyl riv, 2800 S
JONES' CT, E fr 203 Camac
JONES' LA, W fr Del av, S of Av 34th S, & (Pville), E fr Island rd, S of S 76th
JOSEPHINE (Fkd), N E fr Church to Oxford, S E of Tackawanna
JOYCE, N fr E Elkhart to E Clearfield & fr E Schiller to E Venango, W of Fkd av
JUAN PL, E fr 527 S 13th
JUDSON, N fr Shamokin to Noble, 2311 Buttonwood to Brandywine, Aspen to Girard av, & fr Ridge av to Norris, W of N 23d
JULIUS PL, E fr 1005 S 2d
JUNE (W P), N fr Fairmount av to Aspen, & fr Brown to Westminster av, W of N 46th
JUNIATA, W fr O to N 15th, & (N Town), S W fr 4175 Gtn av to N 32d, S of Bristol
JUNIATA (Bdg), S E fr Fkd creek to Del riv, N of Harrison
JUNIATA PARK (33d ward), Cayuga, L, I & Fkd creek
JUNIPER (See N & S Juniper)
JUSTICE CT, W fr 514 N 2d to Buttonwood

K.

K, N fr Ktn av & E Tioga to Strahle, E of J
KALOS (Wiss), N E fr Ridge av to Retta, N W of Sumac
KATER, W fr S Orianna to S 4th, to S 5th to S Schell, S Alder to S Clifton, & E & W fr 615 S 12th to S Broad & fr S Rosewood to Gray's Ferry av, S of South
KATER PL, S fr 1634 Kater
KATES, W fr 812 S 13th to S Broad, fr al r 1418 Catharine to S Mole, & fr 810 S 15th
KAUFFMAN, W fr S Orianna to 811 S 4th, S Reese to Passy'k av,& fr S 22d to S 24th, S of Catharine
KAYSER'S CT, W fr 312 Mascher
KEICHLEIN'S CT, E fr 1137 Oriana
KEICHLINE PL, N fr 1131 Olive
KELLY'S CT, N fr 317 Fitzwater to Pemberton
KENILWORTH, W fr S Del av to 717 S 2d, S Reese to S Fairhill, W fr 714 S Marshall, 710 S 12th to S Broad, & E fr 709 S 15th to S Rosewood

KENNEDY (Bdg), N W fr Garden to Richmond, N of Salmon, & (Fkd), N W fr Tacony to Trenton av, E of Brill
KENNEDY'S CT, W fr 928 N Front
KENNEDY'S LA, N E fr N 19th & Lehigh av to Hunting Park av, W of N 26th
KENNY'S PL, S fr 234 Monroe
KENSINGTON AV, N E fr 2400 N Front & E York to Fkd av, Fk1
KENTON PL, N fr 217 Sansom
KENWORTHY'S CT, N fr 72, Cherry
KENYON (Gtn), N W fr Woodlawn N E of Gtn av
KERBAUGH (N Town), N fr N Broad to 3925 Gtn av, S of Luzerne (See also E Kerbaugh)
KERN, N fr 2057 E Sergeant to E Huntingdon, S E of Coral
KERSHAW, W fr N 17th to N 19th, N 22d to W of N 25th, N 27th to N 28th & (W P) & fr Lancaster av to N 53d, N of Thompson, fr N 60th to N 61st, N of Haverford
KEYSER, N fr Somerset to Indiana, W of N 21st
KEYSER (Gtn), N W fr Logan to 166 Manheim & S E fr Price, N E of Wayne
KEYSTONE (Tacony), E fr Rawle to Princeton, S of Tulip
KIBLEN PL, N fr 145 Green
KILLIAN'S LA (P'ville), E fr Tincum rd, S of Island rd
KIMBALL, W fr 952 S Water to Front, 1012 S 3d to S 4th, 1016 S 6th to S 7th, 1010 Passy'k av to S 8th, S 10th to S Watts, 1012 S 19th to S 23d & fr S 24th to S 25th, S of Carpenter
KING, N fr Hunting Park av to Abbotsford av, E of Stokley
KING'S LA (Hbg), W fr Bristol rd, ab Pennypack la
KINGSESSING AV (W P), S W fr S 42d & Woodland av to Cobb's creek
KINGSLEY (Myk), N E fr Ridge av to Rittenhouse & Magdalena, S of Rittenhouse & W fr Ridge av to Myk av & fr Boone to Cresson, S of Walnut la
KINGSTON, N W fr G, bel P R R, & E fr Richmond to Myrtle, S of E Venango
KINLEY'S CT, S fr 1624 Lombard

RICHARDSON & ROSS, 30th & Race Sts.

CLAIMS AND LITIGATED MATTERS.

KINSLEY'S PL, N fr Manning, E of 253 S 6th

KIP, N fr 283 Tusculum to Indiana, & (Feltonville), fr Tabor rd E of A

KIRBY AV, N fr Oak la, E of N P R R

KIRBY PL, E fr 417 N Darien

KIRK AV, E fr 719 S 6th

KIRKBRIDE (Bdg), E fr Mercer to Del riv

KITCHEN (Roxb), N E fr Ridge av to Magdalena, N W of Roxb

KLINE'S CT, E fr 1307 Lawrence

KLINE'S CT, W fr 920 N 3d

KNIGHT'S CT, S fr 826 Cherry

KNIGHT'S RD (Byberry)

KNIGHT'S SQ (26th ward), S 33d to S 34th, & 41st to 42d aves, S of 40th

KNORR (Tacony), S E fr Fkd av to Del riv, N of Unruh

KNOWLES AV, S fr 2408 Naudain

KNOX (Gtn), N W fr Logan to Manheim, N E of Wayne

KOHL (Bln), W fr Bustleton pk, N of Boileau

KOHLER'S AV (Myk), N W fr Gowen av, along Canal bank

KRAIL (Falls), N E fr Crawford to Indian Queen la, N E of Ridge av

KRAMS (Myk), N E fr Baker to Wilde, ab Dupont & fr Pechin to Ridge av, S E of Leverington av

KREWSTOWN RD (Bln), E fr Pennypack to Lott, N of Dedaker

KRIDER'S CT, N fr 733 Kater

KUHN'S CT, E fr 1211 Randolph

L.

L, N fr Ktn av & E Venango to Strahle E of K

LABORATORY HILL (Falls), N E fr Ridge av, N of Calumet

LAFAYETTE AV (Falls), E fr 3309 Cresson, N of Ainsley

LAFAYETTE PL, N fr 1307 Fairmount av

LAFFERTY'S ROW (Pt Breez), S fr Magazine la & S 30th, n River rd

LAIRD (W P), W fr 882 N 45th to N 46th & fr N 49th to N 50th, N of Parrish

LAKESIDE AV (Oak la sta)

LAMBERT (See N & S Lambert)

LAMBERT PL, W fr 1933 N 21st

LANCASTER AV (W P), N W fr 3209 Market to County line

LANCASTER RD (W P), E fr City line, N of Lancaster av

LANGDON PL, W fr 1308 S American

LANGTON PL (P'ville), E fr Cemetery la, S of Kingsessing av

LANKENAU AV (W P), N E fr N 49th to W Park, N of Midvale av

LANSDOWNE AV (W P), W fr N 52d & Lancaster av to Cobb's creek, S of Haddington

LARA PL, W fr 200 S 11th to S Marvine

LARDNER (Fkd), W fr Del av to Tacony, N E of Benner

LARE (Roxb), N fr Summit av, W of Ridge av

LARGE (Fkd), S W fr Harrison to Arrott, W of Horrocks

LAROS (Myk), N W fr Rittenhouse to Roxb av, N of Magdalena

LATHBURY'S CT, S fr 520 Kater

LATIMER, E fr S Darien, W fr 214 S 9th to S Delhi, S Jessup to S Marvine, 240 S 12th to S Camac, 248 S Juniper to S Watts, 254 S 15th to S Bouvier, S Opal to S 20th, E fr 251 S 21st & W fr S 22d to S 23d

LATIMER CT, N fr 223 Fitzwater

LATONA, W fr 1224 S 7th to Passy'k av, S Alder to W of S 12th, S 13th to S Juniper, S 15th to 1241 Pt Breeze av, S 21st to S 23d, S 25th to S 28th, S 30th to S 31st & S 32d to S 33d, S of Federal

LAUGHLIN PL, N fr 1519 Palmer

LAURA, N fr 2845 Gordon

LAUREL, W fr N Del av to N 3d N of Poplar

LAURENS (Gtn), N W fr Abbotsford to Clapier, Manheim to School, & fr Woodlawn to Chelten av, E of Wiss av

LAURISTON (Myk & Wiss), S fr Penslake to Walnut la, Kingsley to Hermit, E fr Ridge av to Rochelle av, & fr Magdalena to Wiss creek

LAWNTON (Myk), S fr Livezey to Conarroe, E of Ridge av

LAWRENCE (See N & S Lawrence)

LAW'S CT, S fr 218 Christian

LAYCOCK AV (P'ville), S fr S 74th to S 80th & fr S 86th to S 90th, E of Tinicum av

---

ASPHALTUM BLOCKS and TILES.

LAYMAN PL, N fr 715 Ranstead
LAZARETTO RD (P'ville), S W fr Island rd, S of R R
LEADBEATER'S AV, W fr 212 N Juniper to N Watts
LEAGUE, W fr 956 S Water to S 2d, 1024 S 3d to S 4th, S Reese to S Randolph, 1028 S 6th to S 10th, 1024 S 12th to S 13th, 1026 S 19th to S 20th & fr S 22d to S 23d, S of Carpenter
LEAGUE ISLAND RD (continuation of Old 2d st) running S W to League Island
LEAMY (See B)
LEBANON AV (W P), S W fr N 57th, S of Susq'ana av
LEE (See N & S Lee)
LEEDS PL, S fr 1222 Olive
LEES CT (Gtn), E fr 4514 Miller
LEFEVRE (Bdg), S E fr Fkd creek to Del riv, N of Cayuga
LEHIGH AV, W fr 2700 N Front to Schuy'l riv (See also E Lehigh av)
LEICESTER PL (Gtn), fr Baynton, S E of Armat
LEIDY AV (W P), N W fr N 41st & Girard av to N 44th, S of Parkside av
LEIPER (Fkd), N fr Fkd creek to Oxford rd, N W of Penn
LEITHGOW (See N & S Leithgow)
LELAND, N W fr 1643 Francis to Ginnodo
LEMON, W fr 626 N 10th to Camac, & fr 1320 Ridge av to N Watts
LEMON CT, W fr 1312 Fkd av
LEMONTE (Myk & Roxb), W fr Ridge av to Umbria, S of Cinnaminson la
LENA (Gtn), N W fr 55 Wister, Penn to Maplewood av & fr E Chelten av to beyond Centre, E of Gtn av
LENOX AV, W fr 3624 N Broad to N 15th
LEON (Hbg), S E fr Township line to Pennypack creek, N of Craig
LEOPARD, N fr 21 Richmond to E Thompson
LESHER (Fkd), N fr Orthodox to Meadow, E of Paul
LESLIE (P'ville), W fr S 66th to S 69th, N of Greenway av
LETITIA, S fr 116 Market to Chestnut

LETTERLY, W fr 2444 N 13th to N Clarion, & fr N Carlisle to N 15th, N of York (See also E Letterly)
LEUKON (Wiss), S E fr Roxb to Hermit, N of Rochelle av
LEVERING (Myk), N E fr 4377 Main to Mitchell, ab Grape, & Pechin to Mitchell at Grape, & fr Ridge av to Park line, N W of Roxb
LEVERINGTON AV (Roxb), N E fr Wash'n to Wiss av, S E of Hermitage
LEVICK (Tacony), N fr Del riv to G, W of Hellerman, & (Lawndale)
LEWELLEN'S AV, W fr 918 Beach
LEWIS (Fkd), S E fr Ashland to Sepviva, S of Juniata
LEX (W P), N fr Wallace to Lancaster av, W of N 44th
LEYDEN'S CT, E fr 213 N 10th
LIBERTY CT, E fr 245 N 10th
LIMA PL, N fr 643 South
LIME KILN PIKE (Gtn), N fr York rd at Branchtown to C Hill
LINCOLN AV, W fr 724 S Darien
LINCOLN AV (Gtn), N fr Wiss av to Carpenter, N E of McCallum
LINCOLN SQ (P'ville), S fr Greenway av to N Woodland av, W of S 48th
LINDEN (Hbg), E fr Fkd av to Del river, N of Academy rd
LINDEN PL, S fr 1808 Kater
LINDEN PL, W fr 538 N Percy
LINDEN TER (Gtn), S fr 44 Penn
LINDENWOOD (W P), N fr Jefferson, W of N 52d
LINDLEY AV (Gtn), E fr N Broad & Fisher's la to Tacony Creek, N Ruscomb
LINMORE (W P), W fr S 46th to S 47th, S E of Woodland av
LINNEY (Myk), N W fr Umbria to Wright, N E of Cresson
LIPPINCOTT, W fr N Front to N Lawrence, N 13th to Park av, N 17th to N 18th, N 20th to N 24th, N 31st to N 32d, & fr N 34th to N Shedwick, N of Clearfield (See also E Lippincott)
LISSER AV (P'ville), S W fr S 86th to S 90th, E of Crothers av
LITCHFIELD PL, S fr 126 Bainbridge
LITFORD PL, S fr 66 Laurel
LITTLEBOY'S CT, S fr 216 Arch

RICHARDSON & ROSS, 30th & Race Sts.

LIVEZEY (Roxb), E fr Ridge av to Shawmont av, N of Gorgas la & fr Wiss Creek to Wiss av, N of Allen's la

LIVINGSTON, N E fr 1339 E Columbia av to E Palmer, 1340 E Palmer to Earl, E Susq'ana av to E Norris, Anthracite to E Huntingdon, 2553 E Lehigh av to Auburn, Ann to Ontario, & (Bdg), N fr Wilmot to Lefevre, E of Belgrade

LLEWELLYNS AV, W fr 916 Beach

LOCK AV (Myk), W fr 4162 Main, N of Jamestown

LOCK'S PL, E fr 1113 Leopard

LOCUST, W fr S American to 247 S 3d, 236 S 4th to S 6th, S Franklin to S 18th, & fr S 19th to S 25th & (W P), fr S 32d to Cobbs creek

LOCUST AV (Gtn), N E fr Morton to Sprague ab Church la

LOFTY (Myk), S W fr Terrace to Boone, S E of Roxborough

LOGAN (Gtn), S W fr 4900 Gtn av to Morris, bel Seymour (See also E Logan)

LOGAN SQ, W fr N 18th to N 19th & N fr Race to Vine

LOGUE CT, N fr 1729 Tilghman

LOMBARD, W fr 500 S Del av to Schuyl riv & (W P), fr Schuyl riv to S 33d & Locust & fr Baltimore av, W of S 42d to Del County line

LOMBARD ROW, S fr 710 Lombard

LONEY (Fox Chase), N W fr 2d st pk, S of Rhawn

LONG'S AL, E fr S Hancock to S Mascher, S of Queen

LONGSHORE (Tacony), E fr G to Del riv, N of Knorr

LONGSTRETH CT, W fr 274 S American

LOTT (Bln), S E fr Meeting House rd to Starkey, bel Fulmer

LOUD PL, W fr 808 Marvine

LOUDEN (Gtn), W fr Gtu av to N 2d, N of Wyoming av

LOWBER (W P), N fr 3805 Filbert, Olive W of N 38th & fr Mt Vernon to Wallace

LOWE (N Town), W fr 4331 N 15th to N 17th & E fr 4327 N 18th

LOWER MT PLEASANT (Mt A), E fr Wiss av to Stenton av, S of Mt Airy av

LOXLEY PL, N fr 321 Arch

LUCAS, E fr Tyson to Princeton, N of Erdrick

LUDLOW, W fr 14 S 4th to S 6th, S Perth to 15 S 8th, E fr 23 S 10th, W fr 12 S 10th to S 11th, E fr 19 S 13th, W fr S 16th to S 24th, S of Market & (W P) W fr S 30th to S 32d, S W fr 3226 Market to S 33d, S 32d to S 44th, S 55th to S 56th, & fr S 57th to S 58th, bel Market, thence to Cobb's creek.

LUDWIG (W P), N fr Haverford to Pearl, W of Preston

LUKENS AV (P'ville), S W fr Gibson av & S 68th to Island rd

LURAY (F'ville), W fr N Front to Kin & Oxford turnpike, & fr N 4th to N 6th, N of Courtland & (Gtn) fr N 18th to 4635 Gtn av

LUZERNE (N Town), W fr N Front to Hunting Park av, N of pk (See also E Luzerne)

LYCEUM AV (Roxb), N E fr Myk av to Ridge av, N W of Martin

LYCOMING, N fr N Broad to Gtn av, N of Luzerne

LYDIA, S W fr N Hancock to Sophia, N of Van Horn

LYNN AV, E fr 821 N American

LYON AV (P'ville), S W fr Gibson av & S 68th to Island rd

M.

M, N fr Ktn av & E Erie av to Strahle, E of L

McALPIN (W P) (See N. & S. McAlpin)

McATEE, W fr 1542 Cadwallader

McCALLUM (Gtn), N W fr Rittenhouse to Johnson, & fr Hortter to McPherson, N E of Greene

McCANN'S CT, N fr 731 Rodman to Naudain

McCLANE'S AV, E fr 13 S 20th

McCLELLAN, W fr 1818 S Front to Moyam'ng av, S 4th to S 10th, S 11th to S Sartain, S 13th to S Juniper, S 17th to S 21st, & fr S 24th to S 26th, & fr S 30th to S 32d, S of Moore

McCOY'S CT, W fr 920 S 6th

McDEVITT'S CT, W fr 908 S 17th

McDONALD'S CT, W fr 232 N 15th

McFERRAN (N Town), E fr 3847 Gtn av to York rd

McGAW'S ROW, E fr 775 S 3d

SHEET ASPHALT PAVING of all kinds.

McGUIRE'S CT (W P), S fr 3436 Filbert

McILRAVY, S fr 1106 Montrose

McKEAN, W fr Del riv to S Broad, 2000 S

McKEAN AV (Gtn), N fr Clapier to Manheim, S of Morris

McKEE'S, S W fr Stone House la, E of Old 2d to S of Johnston

McKEE'S AV, No. 2, S fr 1318 Lombard. No. 3, W fr 712 N Uber. No. 4, N fr 1313 Carlton

McKENNA PL, W fr 1730 N 27th

McKNIGHT'S CT, S fr 1808 Naudain to South

McMANEMY'S CT, S fr 430 Fitzwater

McMICHAEL (N Town), N fr Hunting Park av to Abbotsford av, W of Fox

McPHERSON (C Hill), E fr 7500 Gtn av

McPHERSON SQ (33d ward), E Clearfield to E Indiana, bet E & F

McPHERSON'S CT, N fr 2223 Hamilton to Ralston

MADDOX PL, E fr 723 S 4th

MADISON, W fr N 20th to 21st, N of Allegheny av (See also E Madison)

MADISON SQ, W fr S 22d to Gray's Ferry av, S of Catharine

MAGAZINE LA, E fr S 31st & Geary

MAGDALENA (Myk), N W fr Rittenhouse to Gorgas la, W of Laros

MAGEE (Tacony & Vol Town), S E fr Cottage to Del riv, bel Unruh & N of Levick, E fr G, N of Hellerman

MAGILTON'S CT, N fr 1339 Kates

MAGNOLIA (Gtn), N fr Penn to Walnut la, & fr Duval to Sharpnack, E of Morton

MAGUIRE'S CT (W P), S fr 3436 Filbert

MAIDEN (Myk), N E fr 4409 Mansion to Silverwood, N W of Levering

MAIN (Wiss & Myk), N W fr Ridge av at Wiss sta to Wash'n, S W of Cresson

MALCOLM (W P), W fr 728 S 51st to S 52d

MALLORY (Myk), N E fr P & N R R to Wilde, N E of Krams

MALVERN (W P), S W fr Haverford to Cobb's creek, W of Rhoads

MANATAWNA (Roxb), N W fr Mill rd to S of Ridge av, N of Port Royal av

MANAYUNK AV (Myk) Roxb & Wiss), N W fr Rochelle av to Hermitage, S W of Pechin

MANDERSON, W fr 1016 Beach to Fkd av

MANGROVE PL, S fr 640 South to Kater

MANHEIM (Gtn), W fr 5100 Gtn av to Wiss av

MANLEY'S ROW (Falls), E fr Shedwick to N 34th, N of Clearfield

MANNING, W fr 268 S 4th to S 6th, S 8th to S Darien, 262 S 9th to S 10th, 248 S Marvine to S 13th, S Juniper to S Watts, S Broad to 263 S 15th, S 17th to 265 S 20th, S 21st to S Van Pelt & fr 250 S 22d to S 25th, & (W P) fr S 59th to S 60th, S of Locust

MANOR (Myk & Wiss), S W fr Seville to Dawson, N E of Terrace

MANSFIELD AV (Pittville), S fr Haines, E of Stenton av

MANSION (Myk), N W fr 160 Levering to Gay S W of Silverwood, 140 Gay to Conarroe, N E of Baker, & fr Leverington av to Cinnaminson la

MANTON, W fr 1112 S Front to Moyam'g av, 1212 S 3d to S 6th, S Marshall to S 8th, S 15th to S 20th, Pt Breeze av to S 23d, & fr S 24th to S 28th, S of Federal

MANTUA AV (W P), N W fr N 31st & Haverford to N 44th

MAPLE (Gtn), N W fr 123 Rittenhouse

MAPLE (W P), W fr S 60th, N of Greenway av

MAPLE (P'ville), W fr S 60th, S of South

MAPLE PL, W fr 521 N American

MAPLEWOOD (Gtn), W fr 5600 Gtn av to Wayne, S E of Chelten av

MARGARET (Fkd), S E fr 4681 Fkd av to Willow, & S E fr Hawthorne to Tacony creek, thence S to P R R to Little Tacony creek, N of Orthodox, thence to Bdg

MARION (Gtn), S E fr Seymour & N W fr Price to 216 Rittenhouse

MARION PL, S fr 516 Christian

RICHARDSON & ROSS, 30th & Race Sts.

MARKET, W fr Del riv to Schuy'l riv, thence to Cobb's creek to Del County line (Dividing line for numbering North & South)

MARKLE (Myk), N W fr Cresson to Myk av, & fr Lauriston to Ridge av, ab Hermit

MARKLE FL, E fr 517 S 2d

MARKOE (See N & S Markoe)

MARLBOROUGH, S E fr 1435 Fkd av to Del riv, N of Crease

MARMION (Falls), W fr 3620 Conrad

MARMION PL, S fr 224 Christian

MARSH AV, E fr 2821 Gtn av

MARSDEN (Tacony), N E fr Robbins to Cottman, N W of Torresdale av

MARSHALL (See N & S Marshall)

MARSHALL (Oak La Sta), S fr Oak la, W of N 6th

MARSHALL RD (W P), S W fr S 50th to County line, S of Chestnut

MARSTEN PL, W fr 1522 Cadwallader

MARSTON, N fr 2709 Thompson to Eyre, Montg'y av to Berks, S fr Diamond to R R, N fr Diamond to Susq'ana av, & fr York to Cumberland, W of N 27th

MARTHA, N fr Berges to E Dauphin, E Susq'ana av to E Cumberland, S of Fkd av, 2133 E Huntingdon to E Lehigh av, W of Trenton av, E Seltzer to E Somerset, Ann to Clementine, & fr Cope to E Virginia, E of Amber

MARTIN (M'ville), W fr Pt House rd, bel Greenville

MARTIN (Roxb), N E fr 4367 Myk av to Wiss Creek, S E of Lyceum av

MARVINE (See N & S Marvine)

MARVINE PL, W fr 1440 N Marvine

MASCHER, S fr 126 Arch to Cuthbert, & fr 141 Girard av to Erie av, & (Olney) fr K & O Turnpike to Chew, W of N Front

MASON (Tacony), E fr Knorr to Tyson, S of Wissinoming

MASTER, W fr 1400 Fkd av to Schuy'l riv, & (W P) N fr Haverford to Lancaster av, fr N 50th to N 63d

MATTIS, N E fr 307 S 2d to 120 Dock

MATTSON PL, E fr 1037 Crease

MATZINGER'S CT, N fr Quarry, W of N 12th, S of Race

MAXWELL'S CT, N fr 1217 Kater

MAXWELL'S CT, S fr 232 Christian

MAY (W P) (See N & S May)

MAYFIELD, W fr N American to N 3d, & fr N Broad to N 15th, N of Indiana. (See also E Mayfield)

MAYLAND (Gtn), N E fr Baynton to Morton, & fr Sullivan to Cemetery, N W of Tulpehocken

MEADE (O Hill), W fr N 27th to N 33d, S of Highland av

MEADLAND AV (W P), S fr Marston to University, W of R R

MEADOW (Fkd), S E fr Fkd av to Ditman, N E of Orthodox

MECHANIC (Gtn), N E fr Carswell to Magnolia, & fr Crittenden to Cemetery, S E of High

MEDARY (Somerville), E fr Stenton av to Limekiln pk, S of E Chelten av

MEDIA (W P), W fr Belmont av to N 50th, & fr N 52d to N 66th, N of Master

MEDINA, W fr 1320 S 7th

MEEHAN (Gtn), N fr 6813 Gtn av to Sprague, N of Pleasant, & (Pittville) fr Mansfield to Woolston

MEETING HOUSE LA (W P), N E fr N 53d to N 52d & Girard av, ab Wynlusing

MEETING HOUSE RD (Bln), N E fr Fox Chase rd to Lott

MEGARGEE (Bln), S E fr Pennypack creek to Starkey, S of Mower

MELINA PL, N fr 417 Naudain

MELON, W fr N 9th to Ridge av, N Broad to N Sydenham, N 16th to N Bouvier, & (W P) N 33d to N 34th, N 35th to N 40th, & fr 650 Lex to N 45th, N of Wallace

MELROSE (Fkd), N fr Lewis to Bridge, S E of Tacony

MELROSE AV, W fr 1070 Fkd av

MELVALE, N fr Sarah & N E fr E William to E Venango, E of Richmond & (Bdg), N E fr Jenks to Kirkbride

MELVILLE (W P), S fr Linmore av to Saybrook, & fr Yocum to Kingsessing av, W of S 45th

MEMPHIS, N E fr E Columbia av to E Erie av, S E of Tulip

ASPHALTUM BLOCKS and TILES.

MENN'S PL, S fr 912 Hamilton

MENTOR (Feltonville), E fr N 3d n Wyoming av

MERCER, E fr 1325 Fkd av to Crease, Norris to Fletcher, E Dauphin to E York, N E fr Anthracite to P & R Rw, W of E Thompson, 2800 E Somerset to Auburn, E of Almond, N E fr Oakdale to E Venango, & (Bdg) S & N fr Orthodox to Buckius, & fr Ash to 3354 Pratt

MERCER PL (Gtn), E fr Rubicam S of Ashmead

MERCY, W fr 2024 S Water to Moyam'g av, S 4th to S 8th, & fr S 10th to S 13th

MEREDITH, W fr 718 N 22d to N 23d, & fr N 24th to N 26th (W P), fr 735 N Markoe to N 47th

MERIDA PL, E fr 763 S Front

MERIDIAN (Hbg), S W fr Walker, N W of Cambridge

MERION (W P), N W fr N 44th to N 52d, N of Lancaster av

MERKES AV, N fr 239 Poplar

MERMAID AV (C Hill), S W fr 7700 Gtn av to Wiss av, N of Hillside av. (See also E Mermaid av)

MERVINE (See N & S Marvine)

MICA (W P), N fr Seneca, W of N 44th

MICHENER (Bln), S E fr Meeting House rd to Starkey, ab Murray

MIDVALE (W P), N E fr Christ Church Hospital to W Park, ab Crestline av, & fr Wiss av to Windemere av

MIDVALE AV (Falls), E fr 4207 Ridge av

MIFFLIN, W fr Del riv to Schuy'l riv, 1900 S

MIFFLIN SQ (1st ward), S 5th to S 6th, Wolf to Ritner

MILDRED (See N & S Mildred)

MILL (Falls), E fr Cresson, N of Midvale av

MILL (Gtn) (See Church la)

MILL (Hbg), N W fr Bln R R to Welsh rd, S W of Pennypack creek

MILL RD (C Hill), N E fr Rex to N 20th

MILLER, N E fr Orange to Emerick, 1419 E Montg'y av to Hewson, N of Belgrade, Aramingo av to E William, Ann to Commissioner, N of E Indiana, E Clearfield to E Ontario, & fr Albert to E Venango, W of Belgrade, & (Bdg) N fr Lefevre to Buckius, bet Belgrade & Fkd creek

MILLETT (Hbg), E fr Cottage, N of Ashburner la

MILLICENT AL, E fr 327 Mascher

MILNOR (Fkd), S fr Bridge to Granite, W of Fkd creek

MINERAL ROW (P'ville), S fr Lyou av, E of Powers la

MINERVA (Roxb), S W fr Ridge av to Eva, S E of Shawmont av

MISKEY (Myk), S fr Levering, E of Ridge av

MITCHELL (Roxb), S E fr Hermitage to Roxb av, fr Gates to Walnut la, fr Markle to Hermit, W of Ridge av

MOEHLER'S CT, E fr 1247 N Front to N Lee

MOLAND AV, E fr 429 N 13th

MOLE (See N & S Mole)

MONMOUTH, W fr 2918 N Hancock to Palethorp, & fr Gtn av to N 11th, N of Cambria
(See also E Monmouth

MONROE, W fr 750 S Front to S 5th

MONTAGUE (Hbg), N fr Rhawn to Mill, E of Erdrick

MONTECELLO AV, W fr N 52d, ab P R R

MONTEREY, W fr 520 N 19th to N 20th, & fr opp 555 Ringgold, to N Randolph, N of Spg Garden, W of N 24th

MONTGOMERY AV, W fr 1800 N Front to N Howard, & fr 1722 Bodine to N 33d
(See also E Montg'y av)

MONTROSE, W fr 924 Moyam'g av to S 13th, 916 S 15th to S 25th, & fr 924 Gray's Ferry av to S 26th

MONUMENT RD (W P), N W fr Belmont av to City av & E of City av

MOORE, W fr Del riv to S 10th, & fr S 11th to Schuy'l riv, 1800 S

MOORE'S AV, W fr 704 N Front

RICHARDSON & ROSS, 30th & Race Sts.

MORAVIAN, W fr 138 S 2d to S American. 132 S 10th to S Clifton, E fr 127 S 12th, W fr S Broad to S 21st, S of Sansom & (W P), 126 S 32d to S 35th, & fr S 36th to S McAlpin

MORELAND AV (C Hill), W fr 7800 Gtn av to Wiss av, N of Mermaid av
  (See also E Moreland av)

MORNEN AV (P'ville), S fr S 86th, E of Lisser av

MORO (Hbg), S W fr Rhawn to Welsh rd, S of Lion

MORRIS, W fr S Del av to S 21st, 1700 S

MORRIS (Gtn), E fr Hortter to Robert's av, S W of Wayne

MORSE, W & S fr 1816 Gtn av to 549 Montg'y av, 1814 N 15th to N 16th, & fr 1802 N 19th to N Uber

MORTON (Gtn), N W fr Church la to Price, N E of Baynton, E Rittenhouse to Haines, E of Gtn av, & fr Haines to Upsal, N W of Pulaski av

MOSS (W P), N fr 4713 Haverford to Fairmount av, & fr Westminster av to Wyalusing, W of N 47th

MOTT, W fr 1002 S 13th to S Watts

MOUNT AIRY AV (Mt A), W fr 7200 Gtn av
  (See also E Mount Airy av)

MOUNT PLEASANT AV (Gtn), N E fr P G & O H R R, S of Mt Airy av
  (See also E Mount Pleasant av)

MOUNT VERNON, W fr 614 N 9th to N 23d, & (W P), N W fr Mantua av to N 40th, N of Haverford

MOUNTAIN, W fr 1630 S Front to Fernon, S 2d to Moyam'g av, S 5th to S 7th, 1633 Beulah to E & W of 1625 S 11th & fr S 18th to S 22d, S of Tasker

MOUSLEY'S CT, E fr 1549 N 4th

MOWER (Bln), S E fr Meeting House rd to Starkey, N of Megargee

MOWER (Gtn), N W fr Carpenter to Cresheim rd, S W of Gtn av

MOYAMENSING AV, S W fr 900 S 2d to S 5th & Jackson (see also W Moyamensing av)

MOYER, N E fr E Columbia av to Palmer fr E Montg'y av to E. Cumberland, E of E Thompson & N W fr 2637 E York to Cedar & E Lehigh av, W of Aramingo canal

MOYER'S LA (Roxb), W fr Ridge av, N of Domino la

MULBERRY (Fkd), N fr Oxford to Bridge, W of Tackawanna

MUNSON'S CT, W fr 738 S 4th

MUREUS PL, N fr 731 Cherry to Race

MURRAY (Bln), S E fr Meeting House rd to Starkey, ab Fulmer

MURRAY'S CT, S fr 640 Bainbridge

MURRAY'S CT, S fr 1130 Spring

MURROW'S CT, S fr 1512 Kater

MUSGRAVE (Gtn), N W fr Church la to Gorgas, N of Chew

MUTTER, N fr 167 Berks to Norris, Colona to Indiana & fr Tusculum, N E of N Hancock

MYERS CT, E fr 241 N 15th

MYRTLE, W fr N Lawrence to N 5th, E & W fr N Warnock, & W fr 846 N 11th to Ontario, & fr 856 N 22d to 871 N 23d
  (See also E Myrtle)

MYRTLEWOOD, N fr Ogden to Poplar, Stiles to Master & fr Dauphin to Cumberland, W of N 29th

N.

N, N fr Ktn av & Butler to Strahle, E of M

NAGELS AV, W fr 342 Mascher

NAHANT, N fr Pike, E of N Marshall

NAOMI AV (Blue Bell Hill), S W fr Wiss av to Leukon, S E of Umbria

NAPA (See N & S Napa)

NAPFLE (Hbg), E fr Bustleton pike to Del riv, S of Decatur

NARRAGANSETT PL (Gtn), S fr 5017 Hancock

NASH (Gtn), N W fr Bellfield to Church la, N E of Bellfield

NASSAU, W fr intersection of Ridge av & N 21st to N 25th, N of Jefferson
  (See also E Nassau)

NATIONAL (Tacony), W fr State rd to Trenton av, ab Friendship

SHEET ASPHALT PAVING of all kinds.

NATRONA, N fr Oxford to Montg'y av, Diamond to Susq'ana av, Ridge av to Huntingdon, & (W P) Race to Powelton av & fr Brandywine to Haverford, W of N 25d

NAUDAIN, W fr 510 S Front to S 2d, 512 S 7th, 508 S 10th to S 11th, E fr 515 & W fr 514 S 15th to S Taney & (W P) fr S 50th to S 52d, & fr S 60th to S 63d, S of Lombard

NECTARINE, W fr N Front to N 2d, N 8th to N 11th, N 12th to N Broad, N 19th to N 20th, N Bucknell to Judson & fr Ringgold to N 25th, N of Buttonwood

NEDRO (Gtn), E fr Stenton av to N 19th, N of Grange

NEDRO AV (B Town), E fr York rd to N 10th, bel Green la

NEFF, E fr Gaul to Del riv, N E of E Oakdale

NELSON (Gtn), N W fr Locust av to Woodlawn & fr Mt Airy av to Gowen, E of Boyer

NELSON TER (W P), E of & parallel with N 40th, N of Filbert

NESTOR (Bln), S E fr Meeting House rd to Starkey, ab Michener

NEVADA, W fr 2244 N 10th to N 12th, N Sydenham to N Mole, E fr 2230 N 26th & W fr 2232 N 29th to N 31st

NEVIN PL, N fr 1307 Carlton

NEW, W fr 242 N Front to N 4th

NEW (W P), S fr Linmore av, W of S 54th

NEW MARKET, N fr 119 Vine to Gtn av

NEW MARKET PL, E fr 819 New Market

NEW MECHANIC (Gtn), E fr 5925 Underhill, N of Haines

NEW QUEEN (Falls), E fr 3319 Cresson, N of Fairview

NEWHALL (Gtn), N fr Apsley, W of Wayne & fr Manheim to Penn, E of Pulaski av

NEWKIRK, N fr Parrish to N of Brown, Stiles to Montg'y av, S W fr Ridge av ab Berks, Diamond to Susq'ana av, & fr Lehigh av to P & R Rw, W of N 28th

NEWLAND, S fr Shawmont av, E of Eminence

NEWTON (C Hill), S fr Stenton av to C Hill & Bethlehem pike, W of Summit

NICE, N fr 18 McFerran to P & R Rw, E of Gtn av

NICETOWN LA, N W fr Front, N of Butler to N 15th, S of Bristol (See also E Nicetown la)

NICHOLAS, W fr N 10th to N 22d & fr N 23d to N 26th, & fr N 32d to Natrona, N of Oxford

NICHOLS AV, N fr 2035 Waverly

NICKELS, Al, E fr 339 Mascher

NINEVEH PL, S fr 424 Fitzwater

NIPPON (Mt Airy), N W fr 7212 Gtn av to Seminole, N of Mt Airy av

NIXON (Myk), N W fr Leverington av

NOBLE, W fr N Del av to N Broad, 432 N 18th to N 19th, 418 N 22d to N 24th & (W P), fr N 61st to N 62d, S of Girard av

NOLEN'S CT, N fr 1435 Parrish

NORFOLK, W fr 850 S. Swanson to S Front

NORMAN (C Hill), S W fr Gtn av, N W of C Hill av

NORRIS, W fr 2000 N Front, to N 33d (See also E Norris)

NORRIS PL, E fr 335 Mascher

NORRIS SQ, N fr Diamond to Susq'ana av, & W fr N Howard to N Hancock

NORTH, W fr N 11th to N 13th, & fr N Broad to N 21st, N of Wallace

N ALDER, N fr Cherry to Quarry, Winter to Vine, Wallace to Melon, Poplar to Montg'y av, Berks to Diamond, & fr York to 2550 Gtn av, W of N 10th

N ALLISON (W P), N fr Market to Arch, & fr Poplar to Oxford, W of N 55th

N AMERICAN, N fr Filbert to Cuthbert, 215 Vine to Gtn av, & fr Master to Venango, E of N 3d, & (Olney), N fr Tabor rd to Grange, S W of N 2d

N BAMBREY, N fr Brown to Girard av, 2521 Columbia av to Montg'y av, & fr Page to Diamond, E of N 26th

N BANCROFT, N fr 1605 York to Cumberland, Clearfield to Lippincott, & fr Allegheny av, & (Gtn), S fr Haines, W of N 16th

RICHARDSON & ROSS, 30th & Race Sts.

EQUITABLE RATES—PROMPT RETURNS.

N BEECHWOOD, N fr Arch to Cherry, Brown to Parrish, Bolton to Oxford, Columbia av to Montg'y av, & fr Dauphin to York, W of N 21st, & (Gtn), N fr Church la to Godfrey, E of Stenton av

N BEULAH, N fr 709 Green

N BODINE, N fr 237 Winter to Wood, N fr r 336 N American, Carlton to Callowhill, 215 Willow to Noble, Buttonwood to Brown. Jefferson to Montg'y av, Norris to Lehigh av, & fr Bristol to Cayuga

N BONSALL, N fr Cherry, W of N 23d, Race to Vine, & fr 1723 N 23d to 2323 Ridge av

N BOUVIER, N fr Quarry to Race, Winter to Vine, North to Fairmount av, Master to Berks, Susq'ana av to Cumberland, Ontario to Estaugh, Venango to Pacific, W of N 17th, fr Wingohocking, W of Colorado, & (Gtn), fr Limekiln pike ab Church la

N BROAD, N fr Market at City Hall to Cheltenham av

N BUCKNELL, N fr Buttonwood to Nectarine, Aspen to Girard av, & fr Montg'y av to Berks, E of N 24th

N CAMAC, N fr 1227 Cherry to Summer, Mt Vernon to Melon, 1223 Brown to Parrish, Thompson to Ingersoll, Master to Susq'ana av, Dauphin to York, & fr Atlantic to Pike, W of N 12th

N CAPITOL, N fr 2025 Market to Commerce, & fr Fairmount av to Parrish, W of N 20th

N CARLISLE, N fr 1423 Cherry to N of 1415 Race, S fr 1416 Vine, 1421 Brown to Columbia av, Norris to Huntingdon, Indiana to 1423 Rush, S & N fr 1414 Allegheny av to Venango, & fr Erie av to Butler, E of N 15th

N CHADWICK, N fr 1631 Olive to Swain, Susq'ana av to Lehigh av, & fr Clearfield to Lippincott, W of N 16th

N CLARION, N fr Appletree to Quarry, Race to Vine, Jefferson to Berks, & fr Diamond to French, & fr York to Letterly, W of N 13th, & S fr Pike

N CLEVELAND, N fr 1809 Girard av to Stiles, Norris to Fontain, Susq'ana av to Cumberland, S fr Indiana, N fr 1813 Cayuga & Limekiln pike

N CLIFTON, N fr Cherry to Quarry, 1035 Spring to Vine, & fr Montg'y av to Berks, W of N 10th

N COLLEGE AV, W fr Ridge av to N Stillman, S of Thompson

N COLORADO, N fr 1707 Susq'ana av to Cumberland, & N & S fr Wingohocking to Blavis, W of N 17th

N CONESTOGA (W P), N fr Market, W of N 54th, S fr Westminster av, N fr Penngrove to Wyalusing, & fr Girard av to Hunters av, W of N 54th

N CROSKEY, N fr Arch to opp 2219 Cherry, S fr 2208 Race, N fr 2215 Summer to Vine, Shamokin to Noble, 2217 Aspen to Brown, Columbia av to Diamond, & fr Somerset to Indiana, W of N 22d

N DARIEN, N fr 817 Race to Buttonwood, Wallace to Fairmount av, Brown to Thompson, Jefferson to Susq'ana av, Huntingdon to Somerset, & fr Indiana av to Clearfield, W of N 8th

N DE KALB (W P), N fr 3721 Cuthbert to Warren, & fr 3709 Fairmount av

N DELAWARE AV, N fr Market to Shackamaxon along Delaware riv

N DELHI, N fr 925 Thompson to Jefferson, Susq'ana av to Dauphin & fr Boston to Cumberland, E of N 10th

N DOVER, N fr 2831 Stiles to Glenwood av, & fr Herman to Cumberland

N EDGEWOOD (W P), N fr Market to Girard av, & fr Master to Lansdowne av, W of N 60th

N FAIRHILL, N fr 529 Cherry to Vine, Montg'y av to Moore, Diamond to Clearfield, Westmoreland to Glenwood av, & fr Pike to Luzerne, & (Oak la), fr 65th to 66th av, W of N 5th

N FALLON (W P), N fr Parrish to Westminster av, W of N 48th

N FARSON (W P), N fr Market to Haverford, Westminster av to Wyalusing, & fr Girard av to Kershaw, W of N 50th

ASPHALTUM BLOCKS and TILES.

N FAWN, N fr Master to Montg'y av, & fr Dauphin to York, W of N 12th

N FELTON (W P), N fr Market to Haverford, W of N 62d

N FRANKLIN, N fr 719 Cherry to Dauphin, York to Lehigh av, & fr Somerset to Clearfield, W of N 7th

N FRAZIER (W P), N fr Vine to Westminster av, E of N 57th

N FRONT, N fr 101 Market to Butler, Luzerne to Juniata, & Cayuga to Cheltenham av

N GARNET, N fr 1914 Jefferson to Oxford, Dauphin to York, & Cumberland, W of N 19th, & fr Cambria to Indiana

N HANCOCK, N fr 153 Willow to Noble, Green to Gtn av, Wildey to Indiana, & fr Tusculum to Ontario

N HARMONY (W P), N fr 3523 Fairmount av to Aspen

N HICKS, N fr 1511 Race, 1515 Morse to Monument cem, 1513 Lehigh av to Mundell, & S fr Indiana, W of N 15th

N HOLLY (W P), N fr Powelton av to Spg Garden, Haverford to Fairmount av, thence N fr Aspen to Westminster av, E of N 42d

N HOWARD, N fr 113 Pegg to Crooked pl, N Hancock to Allegheny av & (N Town) Loudon to Rockland, W of N Front

N HUTCHINSON, N fr 925 Filbert, Cherry to Race, 916 Vine, 917 Callowhill to Noble, 923 Mt Vernon to Melon, 913 Olive to Parrish, 921 Poplar to Columbia av, Diamond to Susq'ana av, & fr 927 Huntingdon to Cambria, E of Gtn av

N ISEMINGER, N fr Quarry to Landreth, & fr Montg'y av to Susq'ana av, E of N 13th

N JESSUP, S fr Winter, N fr 1115 Poplar to Thompson, Montg'y av to Norris, & fr 1117 Cumberland to Oakdale

N JUNIPER, N fr Market to Vine, E of N Broad

N LAMBERT, N fr Cherry to Race, 2037 Master to Sharswood, Jefferson to Redner, Columbia av to Berks, Norris to York & fr Somerset to Indiana, E of N 21st, & (Gtn), N fr Spencer av to Godfrey

N LAWRENCE, N fr Race to York av, 415 Buttonwood to Green, Brown to Gtn av & fr Berks to Cheltenham av, W of N 4th

N LEE, N fr Beach to 8 Brown, 47 Wildey to Girard av, fr S of Thompson to Master & fr Jefferson E of N Front, E fr 2431 N Front to E Cumberland to E Huntingdon, E Somerset to E Cambria, E Clearfield to E Lippincott & fr Wingohocking to Courtland, E of N Front, thence to F'ville

N LEITHGOW, N fr 415 Market to Commerce, S & N fr 417 Poplar, Thompson to Jefferson & fr Cadwallader to Lehigh av & fr Somerset to Allegheny av, W of N 4th

N McALPIN (W P), N fr Aspen to Brown, W of N 36th

N MARKOE (W P), N fr Haverford to Lancaster av, W of N 46th

N MARSHALL, S fr 616 Cherry & N fr Vine to Gtn av, Dauphin to Tusculum, Somerset to Glenwood av & fr Tioga to Luzerne, W of N 6th

N MARVINE, N fr 1121 Race to Vine, Pearl to Wood, Melon to Fairmount av, Brown to Parrish, Thompson to Susq'ana av, Cumberland to Huntingdon & fr Lehigh av to Cambria, W of N 11th

N MAY (W P), N fr 4641 Brown & fr 4641 Westminster av

N MILDRED, N fr 809 Cherry to Race, Spring to 810 Summer & S fr 808 Buttonwood

N MOLE, N fr 1531 Cherry to Race, 1527 Spring, 1513 Susq'ana av to Dauphin & fr York to Huntingdon, W of N 15th

N NAPA, N fr Morse to Berks, York to Lehigh av, & (W P) fr Hamilton to Spg Garden, W of N 31st

N NORWOOD, N fr Somerset to Clearfield, & (Gtn) N fr Church la to Godfrey, W of N 21st

N OPAL, N fr Race & fr Penna av, W of N 19th, 1925 Parrish to Poplar, 1919 Jefferson to Huntingdon, fr Cumberland, W of N Uber & fr Nedro to Spencer, W of N 19th

RICHARDSON & ROSS, 30th & Race Sts.

N ORIANNA, N fr 319 Cherry to Race, Vine to Green, N fr E of 623 N 4th, Brown to Jefferson, Columbia av to Montg'y av & fr Berks to Clearfield, W of N 3d

N ORKNEY, N fr 443 Fairmount to Olive, N & S fr Reno to Myrtle, Culvert to Castner av, Lawrence to Thompson, Master to Oxford. Norris to Clearfield & fr Westmoreland to Ontario, E of N 5th

N PATTON, N fr Turner to Columbia av & connecting R R, Berks to Norris & fr York to Huntingdon, E of N 32d

N PERCY, N fr W of 12 N 9th, 933 Callowhill to Buttonwood, 905 Fairmount av to Parrish, 923 Spg Garden to Wallace, 911 Poplar to Master, Diamond to Susq'ana av & fr Indiana to Glenwood av

N PERTH, S fr 724 Filbert, N fr Arch to Race, 719 Buttonwood to Fairmount av, Parrish to Poplar & fr Thompson to Columbia av, W of N 7th

N PHILIP, N fr 221 Market to Church, New to Vine, N fr 205 Willow, N & S fr Pegg, 207 Buttonwood to N of Green, 213 Master to Huntingdon, Lehigh av to Somerset & fr Tioga to Venango, W of N 2d

N PRESTON (W P), N fr Market to Lancaster av, W of N 40th

N RANDOLPH, N fr 527 Race to Noble, Buttonwood to Fairmount av, Brown to Montg'y av, Norris to Diamond, Edgeley to Susq'ana av, & fr Allegheny av to Butler, W of N 5th

N REDFIELD (W P) N fr Market to Vine, Callowhill to Haverford & fr 5915 Girard av to Lansdowne

N REESE, N fr 509 Cherry to Race, Vine to Summer, fr Columbia av, W of N 5th, Montg'y av to Morse, S fr 512 Norris to al & N fr Norris to Allegheny av, & fr Pike to Luzerne, W of N 5th

N ROSEWOOD, N fr 1419 Clearfield to Allegheny av

N SARTAIN, N fr 1133 Spring to Winter, Poplar to Thompson, Montg'y av to Berks, & fr 1129 Cumberland to Oakdale

N SCHELL, N fr 825 Filbert to Cuthbert, E & W fr Appletree to Cherry, & S fr 830 Vine

N SHEDWICK (Falls), N fr Allegheny av to Hunting Park av, W of N 34th, & (W P), N fr Lancaster av, W of N 34th, & fr Wallace to P R R

N SHERIDAN, N fr Commerce to Filbert, 621 Cherry to Race, Montg'y av to Berks, & fr Dauphin to Cumberland, W of N 6th

N SMEDLEY, N fr 1625 Ingersoll to Master, Susq'ana av to Cumberland, & Clearfield to Erie av, W of N 16th, & (Gtn) fr Plymouth to Cheltenham av

N SPANGLER, N fr Cumberland to Huntingdon & (W P), fr 3307 Race to Powelton av

N STANLEY, N E fr 3029 Ridge av to Susq'ana av, E of N 31st, & fr Columbia av to Glenwood av, W of Corlies

N STILLMAN, N fr 2513 Hamilton to Buttonwood, Brown to Thompson, Jefferson to Oxford, Columbia av to Montg'y av, fr Page & fr Norris to Diamond, W of N 25th

N SWANSON, N fr E Somerset to Gurney, W of A

N SYDENHAM, N fr 1525 North to Melon, Master to Montg'y av, Susq'ana av to Huntingdon, Lehigh av to Mundell, Indiana to Clearfield, & fr Hilton to Pike, W of N 15th

N TANEY, N fr Fairmount av to Thompson, Columbia av to 2612 Montg'y av, & N E fr Montg'y av to Ridge av, E of N 27th

N UBER, N fr Pearl to 1926 Shamokin, Fairmount av to Poplar, Columbia av to Norris, Diamond to Susq'ana av, N fr Cumberland, Westmoreland to Ontario, & fr Ruscomb to Rockland, W of N 19th

N VAN PELT, N fr Cherry to Vine, Montg'y av to York, & fr Somerset to Cambria, W of N 21st

N WARNOCK, N fr 1025 Winter to Vine, 1023 Parrish, Wallace to Melon, 1017 Poplar to Susq'ana av, York to Oakdale, & fr Silver to Cambria, W of N 10th, & fr 66th av N to Lakeside

SHEET ASPHALT PAVING of all kinds.

N WATER, N fr 15 Market to Willow, E Cumberland to E Huntingdon, Gurney to E Somerset, E Clearfield to E Lippincott, & fr E Ontario to E Venango, & (Olney), fr Clarkson to Somerville, E of N Front

N WATTS, N fr Cherry to Pearl, Mt Vernon to Wallace, Parrish to Jefferson, Columbia av to Norris, Diamond to York, Rush to Cambria, S fr Allegheny av, Ontario to Venango, & fr Erie av to N of Butler, E of N Broad

N WENDLE, N fr Quarry to 612 Race, York to Cumberland, fr r of 2615 to r of 2649 N Marshall, W of N 6th

N WOODSTOCK, N fr 2015 Cherry to Race, Brown to Parrish, W of Corinthian av, Jefferson to Redner, Columbia av to York, Allegheny av to Westmoreland, & (Gtn) fr Godfrey to Spencer, W of N 20th

N 2D, N fr 201 Market to Cheltenham av

N 3D, N fr 301 Market to Gtn av & fr 301 Oxford to Cheltenham av

N 4TH, N fr 401 Market to Cheltenham av

N 5TH, N fr 501 Market to Cheltenham av

N 6TH, N fr 601 Market to Cheltenham av

N 7TH, N fr 701 Market to Lehigh av, Somerset to Allegheny av, & fr Ontario to Cheltenham av, thence N fr Oak la

N 8TH, N fr 801 Market to Allegheny av, & Ontario to Cheltenham av

N 9TH, N fr 901 Market to Master & Jefferson, thence to Cheltenham av, & (Oak La), N fr Oak la, W of N & P R R

N 10TH, N fr 1001 Market to Gtn av, & fr Indiana to Cheltenham av

N 11TH, N fr 1101 Market to Clearefild, Allegheny av to Luzerne, & Bristol to Cheltenham av

N 12TH, N fr 1201 Market to Cheltenham av

N 13TH, N fr 1301 Market to Cambria, & Clearfield to Cheltenham av

N 15TH, N fr 1501 Market, to Somset, Indiana av to Gtn av, & Juniata to Cheltenham av

N 16TH, N fr 1601 Market, to Somerset, Cambria to Luzerne, & Bristol to Cheltenham av

N 17TH, N fr 1701 Market to Hunting Park av, & Bristol to Cheltenham av

N 18TH, N fr 1801 Market to N of Fairmount av, Girard av to Huntingdon, Somerset to Luzerene, & Bristol to Cheltenham av

N 19TH, N fr 1901 Market to Huntingdon, Somerset to Luzerene, & Cayuga to Cheltenham av

N 19¾, N fr Cumberland, W of N Opal

N 20TH, N fr 2001 Market to S College av, Master to Cumberland, Lehigh av to Luzerene, & Cayuga to Cheltenham av

N 21ST, N fr 2101 Market to Fairmount av, Brown to Parrish, & fr N College av to Hunting Park av

N 22D, N fr 2201 Market to S College av, & Thompson to Hunting Park av

N 23D, N fr 2301 Market to Poplar, N College av to Diamond, P & R R W to Dauphin, & fr Cumberland to Venango

N 24TH, N fr Winter to Poplar, N College av to Norris, thence to Cheltenham av, W of N 23d

N 25TH, N fr 2501 Callowhill to Poplar, N College av to Diamond, thence to Cheltenham av

N 26TH, N fr 2601 Fairmount av to Thompson, & Master to Ridge av

N 27TH, N fr 2701 Hare to Norris, & Diamond to Hunting Park av, & (C Hill), S fr Willow Grove av, W of Gtn av

N 28TH, N fr 2801 Brown to Berks, & Diamond to Hunting Park av

N 29TH, N fr 2901 Parrish to Hunting Park av, & fr Somerset to Indiana

N 30TH (W P), N fr 3001 Market to Spg Garden, & fr 3001 Penna av to Hunting Park av

N 31ST (W P), N fr 3101 Powelton av to Spg Garden, & fr Penn'a av & Girard av to Glenwood av, & fr Columbia av to Cumberland

RICHARDSON & ROSS, 30th & Race Sts.

N 32D (W P), N fr 3201 Lancaster av to Fairmount av, & fr 3201 Thompson to Hunting Park av

N 33D (W P), N fr 3301 Market to Fairmount av, & fr 3301 Thompson to Hunting Park av, E line of Fairmount Park

N 34TH (W P), N fr 3401 Market to Lehigh av

N 35TH (W P), N fr 3501 Market to P R R

N 36TH (W P), N fr 3601 Market to P R R

N 37TH (W P), N fr 3701 Market to P R R

N 38TH (W P), N fr 3801 Market to Girard av

N 39TH (W P), N fr 3901 Market to Hutton, & fr Pennsgrove to Girard av

N 40TH (W P), N fr 4001 Market to Parkside av

N 41ST (W P), N fr 4101 Market to Parkside av

N 42D (W P), N fr 4201 Market to Mantua av, & Girard av to Parkside av

N 43D (W P), N fr 4301 Haverford to Mantua av

N 44TH (W P), N fr 4401 Haverford to Lancaster av

N 45TH (W P), N fr 4501 Haverford to Wyalusing

N 46TH (W P), N fr 4601 Haverford to Lancaster av

N 47TH (W P), N fr 4701 Haverford to Lancaster av, thence fr Conshohocken av to City line av

N 48TH (W P), N fr 4801 Haverford to Girard av, & fr Jefferson to Parkside av

N 49TH (W P), N fr 4901 Market to Westminster av, Lancaster av to P R R, & Jefferson to Parkside av

N 50TH (W P), N fr 5001 Market to Wyalusing av, Girard av to P R R, & Jefferson to Parkside av

N 51ST (W P), N fr 5101 Market to P R R, & Jefferson to Parkside av

N 52D (W P), N fr 5201 Market to Parkside av

N 53D (W P), N fr 5301 Market to Lancaster av

N 54TH (W P), N fr 5401 Market to Lancaster av

N 55TH (W P), N fr 5501 Market to Lancaster av

N 56TH (W P), N fr 5601 Market to Lancaster av

N 57TH (W P), N fr 5701 Market to Lancaster av

N 58TH (W P), N fr 5801 Market to Lancaster av

N 59TH (W P), N fr 5901 Market to Lancaster av

N 60TH (W P), N fr 6001 Market to Lancaster av

N 61ST (W P), N fr 6101 Market to Lancaster av

N 62D (W P), N fr 6201 Market to Lancaster av

N 63D (W P), N fr 6301 Market to Lancaster av

N 64TH (W P), N fr 6401 Market to Lancaster av

N 65TH (W P), N fr 6501 Market to Lancaster av, & fr Haverford to Lansdowne

N 66TH (W P), N fr 6601 Market to city line

N 67TH (W P), N fr 6701 Market to city line

N 67½ (W P), N fr Haverford, W of N 67th

N 68TH (W P), N fr 6801 Market to city line

N 69TH (W P), N fr 6901 Market to city line

N 70TH (W P), N fr 7001 Market to city line

N 71ST (W P), N fr 7100 Market to city line

N 72D (W P), N fr 7200 Market to city line

NORTHAMPTON CT, W fr 426 Oriana

NORTHWESTERN AV (Roxb), N W of Manatona, n County line

NORTHWOOD PARK (23d ward), Arrott, bet Castor rd & P

NORWOOD (Gtn) (See N Norwood)

NUGENT'S CT, S fr 716 Bainbridge

O.

O, N fr Ktn av & Pike to Strahl, E of N

OAK LA (Gtn), E fr Cheltenham & Willow Grove turnpike to Cheltenham av

OAKDALE, W fr N Wendle to N Marshall, 2634 Gtn av to N 13th, & fr N 15th to N Sydenham, & fr 2653 N 22d to N 29th
(See also E Oakdale)

ASPHALTUM BLOCKS and TILES.

OAKDALE SQ, W fr N 11th to N 12th, N f: Lehigh av to Huntingdon

OAKFORD, W fr 1222 Pt Breeze av to S 23d, S 24th to S 25th, S 27th to S 31st, & fr S 33d to S 36th, S of Federal

OAKLAND (Fkd), N E fr Unitey to Oxford rd, N W of Leiper

OAKLAND PL (Gtn), S fr 218 Duval

OGDEN, W fr 860 N 9th to Ontario, N Carlisle to Ridge av, N 20th to N 23d, & (W P) fr N 29th to N 30th & fr N 39th & Markoe to N 47th, E of Lancaster av, & fr N 49th to N 50th

OGLE (Myk), N fr 155 Fountain, E of Umbria

OLD FRONT ST RD, N E fr Indiana & Boudinot to N Town la, W of Ktn av

OLD PASSYUNK AV, N W fr S 25th & W Passy'k av

OLD 2D, S W fr Mifflin to Buck rd, W of S 2d

OLD YORK RD, N E fr 3241 Gtn av

OLIVE, S E fr 8 Brown to Beach, W fr N Front to Julia, 714 N 4th to N 5th, N Percy to N Broad, N 16th to N 18th, Shirley to N 19th & fr N 22d to N 26th, N of Fairmount av & (W P) fr N 35th to Harmony, N 36th to N McAlpin, Preston to N 41st, W fr Brooklyn, 719 N Markoe to N 47th, & fr N 48th to N 50th, S of Aspen

OLIVE CT, S fr 1312 Olive

OLIVET PL, S fr 1724 Lombard

OLNEY AV (Olney), S E fr Stenton av, S of Chew to Ktn & Oxford turnpike, thence N E to Champlost av

O'NEAL, N W fr 1106 N Howard to 148 Girard av

ONEIDA PL, E fr 805 Mascher

ONTARIO, W fr 3400 N Front to Schuyl riv (See also E Ontario)

OPAL (See N & S Opal)

ORANGE, W fr 236 S 7th to S 8th

ORANGE, E fr 429 Earl to Belgrade

ORCHARD (Fkd), N fr Vandike to Unity, E of Paul

ORCHARD (Gtn), E fr Lena, N of Rittenhouse

OREGON AV, W fr Del riv to Schuyl riv, 2700 S

ORIANNA (See N & S Orianna)

ORKNEY (See N & S Orkney)

ORLEANS, W fr Gtn av to N 11th, N of Cambria (See also E Orleans)

ORMES, N fr E Somerset to E Clearfield, E of B

OROS (Wiss), N E fr Hermit to Wiss drive

ORPHANS RD (Tacony), fr Longshore to Township line rd, E of Wissinoming

ORR, N fr 1815 Francis to Wylie

ORTHODOX (Fkd), N W fr Fkd creek to Asylum rd, E of Duncan

OSBORN (Wiss), N E fr Cresson to Vicaris, N W of Sumac

OSCEOLA (Gtn), S E fr Tulpehocken to Laros & fr 247 Haines to Price, S of Morton

OSMOND (Falls), fr Bowman to Ainslie, S W of Henry

OTSEGO PL, S fr 124 Elsworth to Federal

OTTER (W P), W fr N 39th to N 40th & fr 934 N 42d to N 44th, S of Girard av

OTTO (Somerville)

OTTOMAN PL, E fr 1429 E Clearfield

OTTOWAY PL, E fr 252 Wildey, S of Marlborough

OVERBROOK AV (W P), E & N fr City av to N 58th & W fr Lancaster av to N 66th

OVERINGTON (Fkd), W fr 4732 Fkd av to Leiper

OXFORD, W fr 1600 Fkd av to N 33d & (W P) fr Lancaster av to N 56th & fr N 60th to 70th, N of Jefferson (See also E Oxford)

OXFORD (Fkd), E fr 4521 Fkd av to Tacony

OXFORD RD (Fkd), N W fr 4800 Fkd av to Oxford

P.

P (Fkd), N fr Ktn av to Luzerne to Strahle

PACIFIC, W fr 3640 N Broad to N 15th, N 17th to N 19th, & fr N 21st to N 23d, N of Venango (See also E Pacific)

PACIFIC PL, N fr 1225 Appletree

PACKER, W fr Del riv to Schuyl riv, 3100 S

PACKER PL, N fr 127 Florist

RICHARDSON & ROSS, 30th & Race Sts.

PAGE, W fr N 15th to N 18th, N 19th to N 20th, N Croskey to N 23d, N 25th to Norris, S of Diamond, N W fr Marston to Etting, N E of Sedgley av, N 29th S of Ridge av, & fr N 30th to N 32d, S of Diamond

PALETHORP, N fr 175 Girard av to Master, Jefferson to Montg'y av, Berks to Clearfield & fr Ontario to Venango, E of N 2d

PALETHORP (Olney), fr Chew to Tabor rd, E of 2d

PALLAS (W P), N fr Haverford to Wallace, Aspen to Brown, Ogden to Westminster av & fr 4315 Wyalusing to Mantua av, E of N 44th

PALM (W P), N fr 4111 Parrish to Westminster av

PALMER, N W fr N Front to N Howard, & fr Mascher to N Hancock, N of Columbia av (See also E Palmer)

PALMETTO AV (Lawndale)

PANAMA, W fr 334 S 6th to S 7th, 338 S 12th to S 13th, S Clarion to S Juniper, W fr S 17th, S 18th to S 21st & fr opp 331 S 22d to S 26th

PAOLI AV (Roxb), N E fr Wash'n to Ridge av, S E of Domino la

PARA (C Hill), S W fr Sprague, N W of Abingdon av

PARADISE AV, S E fr Sepviva, bel Wheat Sheaf la

PARK AV, N fr Wallace to Melon, Thompson to Cumberland, Lehigh av to Glenwood av & fr Sedgley av to Tioga, W of N 13th (See also S Park av)

PARKER'S AV (Roxb), S W fr Ridge av, N of Cinnaminson la

PARKSIDE AV (W P), N W fr Girard av & N 40th to N 52d, southern boundary of West Park

PARRISH, W fr N Leithgow to N Lawrence, 846 N 5th to N 17th, N 19th to N 28th & (W P) fr P R R to Haverford, N of Brown

PASCHALL (W P), W fr S 49th & Woodland av to S 50th, S 62d to S 64th & fr S 68th to S 73d

PASSYUNK AV, S W to S Broad & McKean, thence W to Schuyl riv. (W Passy'k av, W of S Broad)

PASSYUNK SQ., S fr Wharton to Reed, W fr S 12th to S 13th

PASTORIUS (Gtn), N E fr 6137 Gtn av to Osceola, N E of Herman

PATTERSON'S CT, N fr 1809 Naudain

PATTON (See N & S Patton)

PAUL (Fkd), S E fr 4623 Fkd av to Vandike

PAXON (W P), N fr Market to Haverford, Westminster av to Wynlusing, Warren to Merion, & fr Jefferson to Columbia av, W of N 51st

PEACH (W P), N fr Race to Vine, N fr Westminster av, Master to Lancaster av, & fr Columbia av to Berks, W of N 53d

PEAR (Fkd), S E fr Mulberry to Tackawanna, N of Gillingham, & fr 4571 Ditman to Race, S of Orthodox

PEARL, W fr 310 N 10th to N Broad, & E & W fr 312 N 15th to Schuy'l riv, & (W P) fr 312 N 32d to N 37th, N 38th to Saunders, N of Powelton av to N 50th, N 54th to N 56th, N 57th to N 58th, & fr N 64th to Simpson, N of Vine

PEARSON (Bln), N W fr Bln pike to Banes, E of Murray

PEARSON AV (Torresdale), W fr Del riv to Fkd & Bristol turnpike

PECHIN (Myk & Roxb), N W fr Hermit to Paoli, N E of Myk av

PEEL, N fr 111 Van Horn to Lydia

PEGG, W fr 446 N Front to N American

PELHAM RD (Gtn), W fr Upsal to opp 6749 Gtn av, S of Carpenter

PELTZ, W fr 2702 Gray's Ferry av to Schuy'l av

PEMBERTON, W fr 738 S Swanson to S 2d, 736 S 3d to S 4th, 724 S Marshall to S 5th, S Mildred to S Schell, S Rosewood to S 15th, & fr 718 S 18th to Gray's Ferry av

PENN (Fkd), N fr Church to Dyre, W of Franklin

PENN (Gtn), W fr 5322 Gtn av to Wiss av, N of Queen (See also E Penn)

PENN CT (Gtn), S E fr Penn, S W of Gtn av

PENN'S CT, W & N fr 1836 Gtn av

SHEET ASPHALT PAVING of all kinds.

PENNOCK, N fr Brown to Poplar. Walter to Stiles, & fr Thompson W of N 27th

PENNSGROVE (W P), W fr N 38th to 41st (Pennsgrove ter, fr N 41st to N 44th), & fr N 54th to N 55th, N of Westminster av

PENNSYLVANIA AV, W fr N Broad ab Callowhill to N 29th, thence to Columbia bridge

PENNYPACK (Bln), S E fr Meeting House rd to Pennypack creek, S of Megargee

PENNYPACK LA (Hbg), fr Bristol rd to P R R, ab Fuller's la

PENROSE AV, S W fr W Passy'k av, W of S 18th to Penrose Ferry bridge

PENSDALE (Myk), N E fr Main to Tower, & fr Terrace to Ridge av, S of Rector

PENTRIDGE (W P), N W fr Florence av to Willows av, ab S 50th

PERCY (See N & S Percy)

PERCY PL, N fr 425 Fitzwater

PERKINPINE'S CT, E fr 721 Mascher

PERKIOMEN, N W fr 1719 Francis to N 19th

PEROT, W fr 710 N 23d to N 25th

PERRY'S CT, N fr 1233 South

PERTH (See N & S Perth)

PETERS, E & W fr 1124 S 12th, & W fr opp 1123 S 23th to S 29th

PHIL-ELLENA (Gtn), S W fr Gtn av to Wiss av, N of Hortter (See also E Phil-Ellena)

PHILIP (See N & S Philip)

PHILIP'S CT, S fr 1740 Lombard

PHYSIC (Gtn), N E fr Baynton, & fr Stenton av to Cemetery, S E of Tulpehocken

PIERCE, W fr 1726 S Front to S 2d, S Philip to 1725 Moyam'g av, S 4th to S 10th, S 11th to S 12th, 1728 Passy'k av to S 13th, & fr S 17th to S 22d, S of Morris

PIERCE (Fkd), N fr Ruan to Margaret, S of Bermuda

PIKE, E fr Roberts av to Ktn av, N of Butler

PILLING (Fkd), N E fr Adams to Unity, E of Wingohocking

PINE, W fr 400 S Del av to Schuyl riv, & (W P) fr Schuyl riv, W to Del County line

PINE RD (Fox Chase), N E fr Old 2d st to Welsh rd, n Abbington township

PIPER'S CT, E fr 617 N American to N Philip

PLEASANT (Gtn), E fr 6801 Gtn av

PLEASANT HILL PARK (35th ward), Linden, bet Del av & Del riv

PLEASANT RETREAT, W fr 636 N 7th

PLUM, W fr Del riv to Richmond, S of E Norris

PLUM (Fkd), S E fr 4619 Hedge to Tacony creek, S of Meadow

PLUSH HILL (Falls Schuy'l)

PLYMOUTH (C Hill), N fr Abington av, E of Gtn av, & fr N 16th to N 17th, N of Av 72, N

PLYNLIMMON PL, W fr 224 N Front

POINT BREEZE AV, S W fr S 20th & Federal to 31st & Geary

POINT BREEZE PARK, Penrose av, Av 38 & Av 42 S

POINT BREEZE PL, N fr W Passy'k av, W of S 28th

POINT HOUSE RD, S E fr Mifflin to Del riv, E of S Swanson

POINT PLEASANT CT, W fr 978 N Del av

POLLARD, N W fr 1016 Front to Allen

POLLOCK, W fr Del riv to Schuyl riv, 3000 S

POMONA (Gtn), W fr Sherman to Wayne, S of Duval

POPLAR, W fr 900 N Del av to Fairmount Park, & (W P) W fr N 38th, S of Girard av, E fr N 41st to P R R, & fr 634 N 52d to N 56th, N of Wyalusing

POQUESSING AV (Torresdale), S W of Grant av, n Del riv

PORT ROYAL AV (Roxb), E fr Schuyl riv to County line rd, N of Rex

PORTER, W fr S Del av to S 30th, S of Ritner

PORTICO (Gtn), S W fr Manheim to Seymour, S W of Gtn av

PORTICO ROW (Gtn), N fr 37 Seymour, W of Gtn av

POTTER, N E fr A to E Huntingdon, B to E Clearfield, & fr G to E Allegheny av, W of Ktn av

POTTERTON HEIGHTS (Gtn), S fr 4714 Magnolia

RICHARDSON & ROSS, 30th & Race Sts.

CLAIMS AND LITIGATED MATTERS.

POTTS, E fr N 4th, N of Wallace, & W fr N 12th to Ridge av, S of Fairmount av
POTTS' CT, W fr 640 N 7th
POWDER MILL LA (Fkd), S W fr Adams to N Town la, W of Leiper
POWELTON AV (W P), W fr 300 N 31st to Market & S 44th, S of Baring
POWERS (Falls), N fr Calumet to Mill, N E of Dobson
POWER'S LA (P'ville), E fr Elmwood av, S of S 72d
PRATT (Bdg), W fr Garden to Fkd creek, S of Bridge, & (Fkd) S E fr Walker to Orchard, W of Granite
PRESTON (W P) (See N & S Preston)
PRICE (Gtn), S W fr Greene to Wiss av, N W of Chelten av, & N E fr 5801 Gtn av to Sullivan
PRINCETON (Tacony), W fr Del riv, N of Tyson
PRISCILLA (Gtn), N W fr Queen to COULTER, E of Morris
PRISCILLA PL, fr 419 South
PRODUCE AV, W fr 418 N Front to N 2d
PROHIBITION AV (Myk), N W fr 4719 Umbria
PROSPECT AV (C Hill), N W fr Graver's la. S W of Stenton av
PROSPECT PL, N fr 1221 Hamilton
PROSPEROUS AL, S fr 1102 Locust
PROVIDENCE CT, N fr 927 Spring
PULASKI AV (Gtn), S E fr Phil-Ellena to Erie av
PULASKI PL, W fr 406 N 23d to Chase pl
PUTNEY (C Hill), N fr C Hill av, W of Norwood

Q.

QUARRY, W fr 140 N Front to W of 146 N 2d, N 2d to N 3d, N 5th to N Sheridan, 146 N Midred, 154 N 8th, 150 N 9th to N Hutchinson, N Alder, E & W to N Clifton, N 11th to N Juniper, N Mole to N 16th, E fr N Bouvier, & fr 145 N 20th, W fr N Croskey to N 23d & (W P), fr N 57th, N of Race
QUAY, S fr Juniata, W of Gtn av
QUEEN, W fr S Del av, S of Catharine to 811 S 6th
QUEEN (Gtn), S W fr 5300 Gtn av to Wiss av
QUEEN AV, S fr 336 Queen
QUEEN ST SQ., 411 to 427 Queen
QUIGG'S ROW, N fr 1019 Hamilton to Buttonwood
QUINCY (Gtn), N fr 224 Allen's la to Gowen av, W of Gtn av

R.

RABBIT LA (W P), S W fr S 52d to Gray's la, S of Chestnut
RACE, W fr 200 N Del av to Schuyl riv, & (W P), fr N 32d to N 36th & Lancaster av, & N 49th to city line
RAILROAD AV (Falls), S E fr Ridge av bel Scott's la
RALSTON, W fr 502 N 19th to N 20th,& fr Penna av to N Stillman
RALSTON PL, N fr 251 Fulton
RANDOLPH (See N & S Randolph)
RANEY'S CT, E fr 405 S 26th
RANSTEAD, W fr 38 S 4th to W of S 5th, 28 S 6th to S 9th, E fr S 10th, 24 S 11th to S 12th, E & W fr 30 S 15th to W of S 18th, 18 S 19th to S 21st, & fr S 23d to S 24th, S of Market
RATIO (Gtn), fr Slocum to Pleasant N of Michener
RAUCH (Fkd), E & W fr Margaret to Tucker, bet Edmund & Adeline
RAWLE (Tacony), E fr Del riv to Emeline, & fr Keystone to Vandike, S of Longshore
RAYNOR (Roxb), E fr 4145 Freeland av
RAY'S CT, E & W fr N Clarion, N of Cherry
REACH, N fr Clearfield to E Allegheny av, & fr Ontario to Tioga, W of G
READING R R & AV, W fr Del riv, N of Lehigh av
RECTOR (Myk), N E fr Canal to Tower, N W of Pensdale, & N E fr Boone to Laros, S E of Roxb
RED LION RD (Byberry), N W fr Academy rd to county line, E of Ashton rd
REDFIELD (W P) (See N & S Redfield)
REDNER, W fr N Leithgow to 1536 N 4th, 1542 N 20th to N 21st, & fr 1534 N 22d to N 25th
REED, W fr Del riv to S 11th, & fr S 12th to S 22d, thence to Schuy'l riv, 1400 S
REESE (See N & S Reese)

ASPHALTUM BLOCKS and TILES.

REGENT (W P), W fr S 42d to S 43d, S 48th to S 49th, & fr S 65th to S 70th, N W of Kingsessing av

REGER (Gtn), S fr Spring al, bel Seymour, W of Gtn av

REICHERT'S CT, S fr 922 Poplar

REID'S AV, W fr 712 S Darien

REIMEL AV (Olney)

REIMER'S AV, S fr 1210 Poplar

REINHARD (W P), N W fr S 47th to S 49th, N of Woodland av, W fr S 71st, S E of Kingsessing av

RENO, W fr 816 N Orianna to N 4th, N Leithgow to N 5th, N 10th to N 11th, 818 N 12th, 814 N 13th to N Broad, N 16th to N 17th, N Bambrey to N 26th, 816 Pennock to N 28th, & (W P) fr N 38th to N 41st, & fr N 48th to N 50th, S of Parrish

RENTSCHLER'S PL, E fr 857 Oriana

RETTA (Myk), S E fr 226 Rochelle av to Wiss, N E of Freeland av

REYNOLDS (Bdg), E fr Richmond to Garden, N of Kirkbride

RHAWN (Hbg), fr Bln turnpike to Del riv, & (Bln), fr Castor's la to County line at Fox Chase

RHOADS (W P), S W fr Haverford to Cobb's creek, S of Malvern

RICHARD PL, S fr 106 Cherry

RICHMOND, E fr 1043 N Front to Fkd av, thence N E to Bridesburg

RICKETTS CT, S fr 210 George

RIDGE AV, N W fr N 9th & Vine to Falls, thence to Myk, Roxb, & Montg'y County line

RIGHTER (Wiss), S fr Ridge av to Sumac, S W of Vicaris

RIGLER'S CT, W fr 1132 Fkd av

RILEY'S PL, N fr Herman, W of N 31st

RING (Myk), N E fr 4365 Main to Levering, N of Grape

RINGGOLD, N fr Buttonwood to Brandywine, 2417 Aspen to Poplar, N College av to Thompson, Montg'y av to Taylor, & fr Norris to Arlington, W of N 24th

RIO GRANDE PL, E fr 1023 Moyamensing av

RIPKA (Myk), S W fr 4614 Ridge av to Myk av & fr 4633 Umbria to Wilde, N of Leverington av

RIPTON PL, W fr 946 N 3d

RISING SUN LA, N E fr Old York rd to Nicetown la & N 5th

RITCHIE (Myk), N fr Green la to Dupont, W of Wilde

RITNER, W fr Del riv to Schuyl riv, 2400 S

RITTENHOUSE (Gtn), S W fr 5900 Gtn av to Wiss creek (See also E Rittenhouse, Gtn)

RITTENHOUSE (Roxb), N E fr Ridge av to Wiss creek, N of Walnut la

RITTENHOUSE PL (Gtn), r 15 Rittenhouse

RITTENHOUSE SQ, W fr 258 S 17th to 261 S 23d, S of Locust

RITTER, N fr E Norris to E Dauphin, & fr Harold to Moyer, S E of Cedar

ROACH'S CT, S fr 1106 Oxford

ROBBINS (Tacony), E fr G, N of Devereaux

ROBERTS AV (Gtn), S W fr 4420 Gtn av to N 34th & P R Rw

ROBIN AV, E fr 707 S Snell

ROBINSON (W P), N fr Market to Lansdowne av, W of N 61st

ROCHELLE AV (Myk), N E fr Cresson to Gorgas

ROCKLAND (Gtn), E fr Gtn av to N 2d, N of Louden

RODMAN, W fr S Philip to S American, S Bodine to S 3d, S Reese to S 8th, S 9th to S Broad, E fr 521 S 15th, S 15th to S 18th & fr 528 S 19th to S 22d

RODNEY (Falls), E fr Ferry, S W of Ridge av

ROMAIN (Fkd), N W fr Ruan to Deal, W of Fkd av

RORER, N fr 527 E Cambria to E Clearfield, W of D

ROSCOE (Falls), S W fr Ridge av to Schuyl riv, ab Calumet

ROSCOE CT, S fr 212 Poplar

ROSE GLEN AV (W P), S fr South to Christian, W of S 63d

ROSEHILL, N fr E Somerset to E Clearfield, W of C

ROSEWOOD (See N & S Rosewood)

ROSINA (Roxb), N W fr Rittenhouse to Stanton, E of Ridge av

ROSS (Gtn), S fr E Phil-Ellena to Upsal, W of Musgrave

ROSS CT, W fr 518 S 23d

ROSSMORE, N fr Tusculum, E of Rosehill

RICHARDSON & ROSS, 30th & Race Sts.

ROTH'S AV, W fr 1320 Gtn av

ROUMFORT AV (Mt A), E fr 7601 Gtn av to township line

ROWAN (N Town), S W fr 4330 Gtn av to Tacoma

ROWLAND (Hbg), N E fr Rhawn, ab Crispin

ROXBOROUGH (Myk), N fr 2459 Main to Terrace, N W of Rector, Rector & (Roxb), W fr Wiss av to Myk av, ab Walnut la

ROXBOROUGH (N Town), N E fr Roberts' av to Fkd creek, N of Luzerne

ROY (N Town), N E fr 3201 Gtn av to Goodman, S of Westmoreland

RUAN (Fkd), E fr Fkd creek to Paul, S of Church

RUBICAM (Gtn), N W fr Shedaker to Bringhurst n P & R R W

RUBICAM PL, N fr 929 Noble

RUDOLPH AV, S fr 730 Race

RUFE (Gtn), N fr 461 Wister to 282 Hermitage

RUFFNER (N Town), Gtn av to N 16th, & fr Blabon to Schuyler, N of Hunting Park av

RULE PL, E fr 743 S 5th

RUPERT (Olney), N fr Castor's la to Ryan

RUPERT PL, W fr 520 N 3d

RUSCOMB (Gtn), E fr E Logan to M, N of Rockland

RUSH, W fr N Marshall to N 7th, N 12th to Glenwood av, N of Indiana av (See also E Rush)

RUSSELL, E fr N 10th to P & R Rw, N of Ontario (See also E Russell)

RUSSELL'S AV, N fr 1541 Parrish

RUTH, N W fr P & R Rw to E Clearfield, & fr Atlantic to P R R, S E of Ktn av

RUTLEDGE AV, N fr E Cambria to E Indiana, E of C

RUTTER'S CT, N fr 205 Federal

RYAN (Fkd), W fr Fkd & Bristol turnpike to Strahle, N of Township line

RYAN'S CT, E fr 1735 Tilghman

S.

SABULA PL, N fr 809 Summer

SACKETT (Fkd), N E fr Bristol turnpike to Colebaugh

SAFFRON PL, S fr 902 Ogden

ST ALBANS, W fr 784 S Swanson to S Front, 756 S 7th to S 8th, 746 S 12th to S 13th & fr 720 S 20th to S 22d

ST BERNARD (W P), N fr Market to Arch & fr Girard av to Thompson, W of N 49th

ST . BERNARD PL (W P), S fr Springfield av to 4913 Chester av

ST DAVID'S (Myk), N W fr Gay to Connarroe, Green la to Carson & fr Ripka to Wright, S W of Mansion av

ST JAMES, W fr 224 S 2d to E & W of S American, S 5th to S 6th, 204 S 7th to 223 S 8th, E fr 217 S Darien, W fr opp 217 S Alder, to S Clifton, 204 S 11th, 212 S 12th to S 13th, 224 S 16th to S 17th, S Woodstock to W of S 20th, & fr S 21st to S 23d, & (W P), W fr S 32d to S 33d & fr S 59th to S 60th, N of Locust

ST JOHN'S PL, E fr 417 N American

ST LUKE'S PL, E & W fr N 16th to N 17th, N of Bristol

ST MARK'S (W P), S fr 4218 Walnut to Locust, Spruce to Pine & S E fr Woodland av, W of S 42d

ST MARTIN'S LA (C Hill), W fr Springfield av, S of Tacoma

ST PAUL'S SQ, W fr 4318 N 16th N of Bristol

ST VINCENT (Tacony), E fr Bustleton pk to Del riv, S of Township Line rd

ST VINCENT PL (Gtn), S fr Chew, E of Woodlawn

SALEM (Fkd), N fr 15 Tacony to Ruan, E of Fkd av

SALFORD (W P), W fr Callowhill to Haverford, W of N 59th

SALMON, S fr 1030 Earl, N E fr 1017 E Palmer to E Eyre, E York to Kirkbride, N W of Richmond & (Bdg) N E fr Fkd av to Pratt, E of Stiles

SALTER, E fr 923 S 2d, 908 S 3d, W fr 906 S 7th to S 8th, 910 S 9th to S Percy & fr 916 S 10th to S Clifton

SAMUELS PL (W P), N fr Haverford, W of N 52d

SANDEL AV, W fr 1034 N 4th

SANGER (Fkd), S E fr Bristol turnpike, N of Dark Run la

SHEET ASPHALT PAVING of all kinds.

SANSOM, W fr S Front to S Amer-
ican, S 4th to S 5th & S 6th to
Schuyl riv, & (W P), fr S 32d to
S 33d, & fr S 34th to Del county
line, S of Chestnut
SARAH, S W fr Wildey to Beach,
E of Fkd av
SARTAIN (See N & S Sartain)
SAUER'S CT, E fr 1415 Randolph
SAUL'S LA, E fr Bln pk, N of
Township line rd
SAUNDERS (W P), N fr Filbert to
Lancaster av, E of N 39th
SAXON PL, S fr 328 Pemberton
SAYBOLT'S CT, N fr 221 Noble
SAYBROOK (W P), W fr Melville
to 1323 S 46th, & fr E of 1415
S 49th to S 50th & fr S 63d to
S 64th, N of Paschall av, & S W
fr S 64th to S 72d, S E of Wood-
land av
SCATTERGOOD (Fkd), S E fr El-
wyn to James, E of Bridge
SCHELL (See N & S Schell)
SCHILLER, W fr N 8th to N 9th,
& fr P & R Rw to N 11th, S of
Tioga (See also E Schiller)
SCHOFIELD'S AL (Myk), W fr 4178
Main
SCHOOL (Gtn), W fr 5500 Gtn av
to Wiss av
SCHOOL (Roxb), N fr Ferry to
Spring, W of Ridge av
SCHOOL AV (W P), S fr 3438
Chestnut
SCHOOL HOUSE LA (Roxb), E fr
Ridge av to Wiss av, bel Wiss
SCHOOL RD (Fox Chase)
SCHURZ (Mt A), N fr Allen's la
to Gowen av, N of Emlen
SCHUYLER (Gtn), N W fr Hunting
Park av to Manheim, & fr Hans-
berry to Queen, N E of Wiss av
SCHUYLKILL AV, S fr South st
Bridge, r U S Naval Asylum, &
along banks of Schuy'l riv, S to
Government av
SCHUYLKILL RD (Roxb), N fr
Domino la to County line, E of
Schuy'l riv
SCOTT'S LA (Falls), N fr Ridge
av to Indian Queen la, W of N
35th
SCOTT'S PL, N fr 1809 Kater

SEARS, W fr 1310 S Howard to
S Hancock, S Philip to S Ameri-
can, 1312 S 3d to Earp, S 6th
to S 9th, S 21st to S 23d, & fr
S 36th to Schuy'l av, S of Whar-
ton
SEDALIA, N fr Luzerne, W of
Richmond
SEDGLEY, S. W fr N 2d &
Erie av to N Broad, N 16th &
Cambria to Montg'y av, W of N
30th, N W of Connecting R R &
parallel therewith
SEDGWICK (Gtn), S W fr 7000
Gtn av to Greene, S of Mt Pleas-
ant av (See also E Sedgwick)
SEISER'S CT, S fr 146 Race
SELFRIDGE PL, N fr 1119 Bain-
bridge
SELLERS (Fkd), W fr Oxford to
Oakland, S of Orthodox
SELTZER, W fr 2746 N 9th to N
Hutchinson, N 13th to N Broad,
2756 N 15th to N 16th, & fr N
26th to N 27th, N of Lehigh av
(See also E Seltzer)
SENATE, W fr 722 S Rosewood to
S 15th, & fr S Hicks to S Mole,
N of Catharine
SENECA CT, W fr 454 Bodine
SENNEFF AV, W fr 638 Camac
SEPVIVA, N fr E Palmer to E
Eyre, 1657 Vienna to E Lehigh av,
& fr E Ontario to Fkd creek, E
of Trenton R R
SERGEANT, W fr N Philip to N
American, 2524 N 12th to N 13th,
N 15th to N Sydenham, N 22d to
N 27th, N of Cumberland, &
(W P) fr N 32d to N 34th
(See also E Sergeant)
SEUBERT'S CT, E fr 1649 Gtn av
SEVIER (Gtn), N W fr Roberts'
av to Manheim, N of Schuyler
SEVILLE (Myk), N E fr Cresson to
Terrace, N W of Hermit, & fr
Myk av to Leukon
SEYBERT, W fr 1326 N 12th to
N 13th, 1312 N 15th to 1309 N
19th, & fr 2021 N College av to
W of N 25th
SEYMOUR (Gtn), W fr 5000 Gtn
av to Morris (See also E Seymour)
SHACKAMAXON, S E fr Fkd av &
E Thompson to Del riv, S of Day
SHAEFER'S CT, S fr 455 Reno, W
of Lawrence
SHAFFER'S AV, S fr 420 Cherry

RICHARDSON & ROSS, 30th & Race Sts.

SHAKER'S AL, S fr 534 Bain-bridge
SHALKOP (Roxb), S fr 539 Hermitage, E of Ridge av
SHAMOKIN, W fr 1016 Ridge av to 409 N 11th, 410 N 18th to N 20th, & fr N 21st to W of N 23d
SHARP (Wiss), S E fr Hermit to Dawson, S W of Terrace
SHARP'S AV, S fr 1222 St James
SHARPNACK (Gtn), W fr Gtn av to Wiss av, N of Upsal (See also E Sharpnack)
SHARSWOOD, W fr N 18th to N 26th, & (W P), W fr N 54th, & fr N 54th to N Conestoga, S of Jefferson
SHAWMONT AV (Roxb), E fr Schuyl rd to Wiss creek, S of Port Royal av
SHAWNEE (C Hill), N W fr Abington to Hartwell, fr Hampton to Bell's Mill rd, S W of Gtn av
SHEAF'S LA, S fr Penrose Ferry rd, S of Magazine la
SHEDAKER (Gtn), N E fr Wakefield to P & R Rw & Duncannon, W of E Logan
SHEDWICK (W P) (See N & S Shedwick)
SHEKINAH AV, W fr 916 Orkney
SHELBURNE AV (Lawndale)
SHELDON (Gtn), N W fr Shedaker to Wister ab Baynton
SHELDON (Myk), N & S fr 238 Wright, & fr Ripka to Fountain
SHERIDAN (See N & S Sheridan)
SHERMAN (Gtn), fr Wash'n av to McPherson av, S W of Green
SHERWOOD (W P), N W fr N 63d, S of Overbrook av, & fr N 73d to Cobb's creek, N W of Columbia av
SHIELDS (P'ville), N fr Woodland av to Greenway av, W of S 66th
SHIELDS' CT, N fr 1231 Catharine
SHIRLEY, S E fr 723 N 19th to 1811 Fairmount av, & (Gtn) N fr Haines, E of N 19th
SHIVELEY'S AV, E fr 819 Camac
SHUNK, W fr Del riv to Schuy'l riv, 2600 S
SHUR'S LA (Gtn), N fr 240 Allen's la to Gowen av, W of Quincy
SICKELS (W P), N fr 5423 Haverford to Westminster av
SIDDALL (Roxb), N W fr Manatawna to Shingle, N E of Tripple
SIDMOUTH PL, N fr 1829 Spruce

SIGEL, W fr 1826 S Front to Moyam'g av, E & W fr S 5th, S 6th to S 10th, 1824 S 11th, 1824 S 13th to S Juniper, S 18th to S 21st, & fr S 24th to S 26th, S of Moore
SILVER, W fr 2723 N 9th to N Broad, & fr N 26th to N 27th, N of Lehigh av (See also E Silver)
SILVERWOOD (Myk), fr Robeson to Roxborough, N E of Cresson, Cotton to Domino, & fr Shawmont to Port Royal
SIMONS LA, E fr S 2d, N of Stone House la
SIMPSON (W P), N fr Race to Girard av, W of N 64th
SIMPSON'S CT, W fr 926 S Front
SINER'S LA, E fr Ktn av to Jasper, N of Pacific
SIXTH ST AV, W fr 1332 N Randolph
SIXTY-FIFTH AV (Pittville)
SIXTY-SIXTH AV N (Oak la), W fr N 5th, S of Independence av
SKERRETT'S CT, S fr 906 Delhi
SLOAN (W P), N fr Filbert to Lancaster av, Fairmount av to Brown, Parrish to Mantua av, & fr Poplar to Eaglesfield, E of N 40th
SLOCUM (Gtn), E fr Gtn av to Sprague, & fr Michener to Pickering, S of Pleasant
SMEDLEY (See N & S Smedley)
SMICK (Myk), N W fr Green la to Dupont, N E of Baker, & S E fr 128 Ripka to Leverington av, & N W fr Hermitage to Prospect, N E of Umbria
SMITH'S AV, W fr 414 S Hutchinson
SMITH'S AV, W fr 1408 N Philip to N American
SMITH'S CT, W fr 1426 N Front
SMITH'S CT, W fr 604 S Juniper
SMITHERS, E fr 3081 Collins to Martha
SNYDER AV, W fr Del riv to Schuyl riv, 2100 S (not open W of S 19th)
SNYDER'S CT, S fr 1218 Pearl
SOBER'S AL, N fr 415 Walnut
SOLLADAY'S CT, N fr Oakdale, W of Melvale
SOLLY (Fox Chase & Hbg), S E fr Montg'y County line, N E of Stanwood av

ASPHALTUM BLOCKS and TILES.

SOMERSET, W fr 2800 N Front to Schuy'l riv (See also E Somerset)

SOMERTON PIKE (Bln)

SOMMERFIELD PL, N fr 331 Green

SOPHIA, N fr 141 E Wildey to Edward

SOUTH, W fr 600 S Del av to Schuyl riv, to S 34th & fr S 44th to Del County line

S ALDER, S fr 1008 Sansom to Moravian, N fr 1009 & S fr 1006 Locust to Spruce, South to S of Fitzwater, 1002 Christian to Salter, 1022 Wash'n av to Ellsworth, Federal to Reed, N fr 1013 & S fr 1014 Mifflin to McKean & fr Wolf to Porter, W of S 10th

S ALLISON (W P), S E fr 5530 Woodland av to Paschall av

S AMERICAN, S fr Chestnut to Dock, Chancellor to De Lancey, Gaskill to Monroe, N fr Catharine, 206 Carpenter & fr Manton to Reed, W of S 2d

S BAMBREY, S fr 2522 South to Bainbridge & fr Webster to Catharine, W of S 22d

S BANCROFT, S fr 1608 Bainbridge to Fitzwater, 1620 Reed to Snyder av, Cantrell to Jackson & fr Wolf to Porter, W of S 16th

S BEECHWOOD, S fr Sansom, W of S 21st, & fr 2122 Dickinson

S BEULAH, S fr Montrose to Carpenter & fr Reed to Mountain, W of S 7th

S BODINE, S fr 238 Market to Ludlow, Ionic to Dock, 236 De-Lancey, Gaskill to Rodman, Christian to S of Carpenter & fr Ellsworth to Federal, W of S 2d

S BONSALL, S fr Chancellor to Locust, Ionic to Walnut, Montrose to Carpenter & fr Federal, W of S 23d

S BOUVIER, S fr Locust to Irving, De Lancey to Pine, Carpenter to Wash'n av, Wharton to Tasker, Mifflin to W Passy'k av & fr Jackson to Porter, W of N 17th

S BROAD, S fr 1426 Market to League Island

S BUCKNELL, S fr Federal to Wharton, W of S 23d

S CAMAC, N fr 1211 Ranstead, 1214 Walnut to Lombard, Titan to Wharton, Dickinson to Pear, N & S fr Tasker to Morris, Moore to McKean & fr Ritner to Porter, W of S 12th

S CAPITOL, S fr 2026 Pine to Addison, Wharton to Reed & fr Dickinson to Tasker, W of S 20th

S CARLISLE, S fr 1414 Pine to Lombard, Ellsworth to Tasker, Moore to Mifflin, Snyder av to Jackson & fr Porter to Shunk, W of S Broad

S CHADWICK, S fr Cypress to 1625 Pine, Bainbridge to Catharine, Carpenter to Wash'n av, Wharton to McKean, W Passy'k av to Jackson, & fr Wolf to Porter, W of S 16th

S CLARION, S fr South to Catharine, N & S fr Federal to Morris, 1314 Jackson to Wolf & fr 1312 Ritner to W Moyam'g av. W of S 13th

S CLEVELAND, S fr 1802 Fitzwater to Catharine, 1802 Carpenter to Wash'n av, Ellsworth to Federal, Wharton to Earp, & fr Dickinson to Snyder av, W of S 18th

S CLIFTON, S fr Ludlow, 1028 Sansom to Walnut, N & S fr Irving, W of S, 10th, Chancellor to St James, South to S of Catharine, Salter to Carpenter, & fr Wash'n av to Ellsworth, W of S 10th

S COLLEGE AV, S W fr Ridge av to Poplar, E of Ringgold

S COLORADO, S fr 1706 Bainbridge to Fitzwater, Carpenter to Wash'n av, Wharton to 1715 Tasker, Mifflin to Snyder av, & fr W Passy'k av to Ritner, W of S 17th

S CONESTOGA (W P), S fr Woodland av to Paschall av, W of S 54th

S CROSKEY, S fr 2212 Chestnut to Sansom, & fr 2218 Pine to Lombard

S DARIEN, S fr 818 Walnut to Spruce, Kenilworth to Pemberton, Fitzwater to Montrose, Wash'n av to S of Alter, Ellsworth to 829 Federal, S fr Reed, McKean to Snyder av, & fr Jackson to W Moyam'g av

RICHARDSON & ROSS, 30th & Race Sts.

S DE KALB (W P), S fr 3714 Walnut to Locust

S DE LANCEY CT, S fr 2048 Lombard

S DELAWARE AV, S fr Market along Del riv

S DELHI, S fr De Gray to Ranstead, Locust to Irving, South to Bainbridge, Fitzwater to Montrose, Ernst to Ellsworth, & fr Wolf to Moyam'g av, W of S 9th

S DOVER, S fr Federal to Oakford, W of S 28th

S EDGEWOOD (P'ville), S fr Elmwood av, W of S 60th

S FAIRHILL, S fr Addison to 529 Lombard, N fr 527 Rodman, W of S 5th, S fr Kater to Senate, Montrose to League, Wharton to Reed, Tree to Wolf, & Ritner to Porter, W of S 5th

S FALLON (W P), S fr 4815 Gray's Ferry av to Paschall av, W of S 48th

S FARSON (W P), S fr Greenway av to Woodland av, W of S 50th

S FAWN, S fr Manning to Panama, N fr 1221 South, & fr Kenilworth to Fitzwater, W of S 12th

S FELTON (W P), S fr Market, W of S 62d

S FRANKLIN, S fr Walnut to Irving, Naudain to Rodman, 712 Wash'n av & fr Reed to Tasker, W of S 7th

S FRAZIER (W P), S fr Hoffman av to Willows av, W of S 56th

S FRONT, S fr 100 Market to Snyder av

S GARNET, S fr 1920 Fitzwater to Catharine, Wharton to Reed, Dickinson to Tasker, & fr McKean to Jackson, W of S 19th

S HANCOCK, S fr 119 Walnut to Sansom, Gaskill to Bainbridge, Catharine to Christian, 130 Manton to Reed, Fernon to Mountain, & fr McKean to Jackson, E of S 2d

S HARMONY (W P), S fr 3442 Sansom

S HICKS, S fr 1512 Market to Ranstead, Spruce to Pine, Waverly to Addison, Bainbridge to Catharine, N & S fr Federal to Ellsworth, Wharton to McKean, Snyder av to Jackson & fr Wolf to Porter, W of S 15th

S HOLLY (W P), N fr Chester av, W of S 41st

S HOWARD, N fr 107 De Lancey, S fr opp 105 Gaskill, Queen to Christian, S fr Carpenter, 112 China, Alter to Ellsworth, Manton to Dickinson, & fr Snyder av to Jackson, W of S Front

S HUTCHINSON, S fr 912 Walnut to Spruce, Pine to Lombard, Fitzwater to Christian, McKean to Snyder av, & fr Wolf to W Moyam'g av, W of S 9th

S ISEMINGER, S fr 1222 Cypress to Panama, 1228 Addison to Lombard, Fitzwater to Kenilworth, N fr Wharton, S fr Dickinson to Pierce, Mifflin to McKean, 1224 Snyder av to Jackson, & fr Ritner to Porter, W of S 12th

S JESSUP, S fr Locust, W of S 11th, Waverly to 1111 Lombard, Bainbridge to Catharine, Montrose to Hall, S fr E of 1121 S 12th, N fr 1107 Morris, S fr Mifflin to McKean, & fr 1112 Ritner to Moyam'g av

S JUNIPER, S fr Market to Catharine, Ellsworth to S of Federal, N fr 1319 Wharton, & S fr Reed to Morris, Moore to Wolf, & fr Ritner to Shunk, W of S 13th

S LAMBERT, S E fr 1317 Pt Breeze av to 2037 Reed, & fr 2036 Dickinson to Tasker

S LAWRENCE, S fr 416 Spruce to Pine, 418 Catharine to Queen Titan to Wharton, Earp to Reed, & fr Gerritt to Wilder, W of S 4th

S LEE, N fr 37 Reed & S & N fr Morris to Hoffman

S LEITHGOW, S fr 413 Walnut, 406 Gaskill to Monroe, 402 Catharine to Queen, Carpenter to Wash'n av. Titan to 415 Wharton, Earp to Reed, & fr Tasker to Morris

S McALPIN (W P), S fr 3036 Sansom to Locust, W of S 36th

S MARKOE (W P), S fr Market to Sansom, Springfield av to Baltimore av, & fr Woodland av to Llumore av, W of S 46th

S MARSHALL, S fr 616 Market to Ranstead, 612 Kater to S of 614 Fitzwater, 610 Wash'n av to Wharton, 606 Dickinson to Tasker, & fr 612 Wolf to Ritner

SHEET ASPHALT PAVING of all kinds.

SHRIVER, BARTLETT & CO. {ADJUSTMENTS
COLLECTIONS

S MARVINE, S fr 1112 Walnut to Lombard, South to Kater, & fr Bainbridge to Catharine, W of S 11th

S MAY (W P), S fr Paschall to Linmore av, W of S 46th

S MILDRED, S fr 814 Bainbridge to Christian, N fr 809 Latona, S fr 804 Reed, McKean to Snyder av, & fr 814 Jackson to W Moyam'g av, W of S 8th

S MOLE, S fr 1522 Market to Ranstead, N fr Spring, S fr Bainbridge to Webster, Ellsworth to Federal, Wharton to Porter, W of S 15th

S NAPA, S fr Gray's Ferry av to Reed, W of S 31st

S NORWOOD, S fr 2112 Dickinson

S OPAL, S fr Locust to Panama, Waverly to Lombard, 1924 Fitzwater to Catharine, 1930 Wharton to Reed, Dickinson to Tasker, & fr McKean to Jackson, W of S 19th

S ORIANNA, S fr 316 Market to Harmony ct, Willings al to Spruce, South to Bainbridge, Kauffman to Queen, Montrose to Carpenter, Sears to Earp, Gerritt to Wilder, & fr Morris to Sigel, W of S 3d,

S ORKNEY, S fr Morris to Tasker, E of S 5th

S PARK AV, S fr 1326 Fitzwater to Catharine

S PATTON, S fr Gray's Ferry av to Reed, E of S 32d

S PENN SQ. W fr S Juniper to S 15th, S of Market

S PERCY, S fr South to Bainbridge, 910 Fitzwater to Christian, Salter to Montrose, S fr Reed to Wilder, Emily to 915 Snyder av, & fr Wolf to W Moyam'g av, W of S 6th

S PERTH, S fr Ludlow to Ranstead, S fr St James, 726 Addison to Lombard, Kater to Bainbridge, N fr Pemberton, & S fr Fulton to Catharine, W of S 7th

S PHILIP, N fr Sansom, S fr Spruce to S of De Lancey, Gaskill to S of Bainbridge, Manton to S of Gerritt, Pierce to bel Moore, & fr McKean to Jackson, W of S 2d

S PRESTON (W P), S fr De Lancey to Pine, W of S 40th

S RANDOLPH, S fr 515 Locust to St James, 524 Lombard to Kater, Kenilworth to Fulton, & fr Carpenter to Federal, W of S 5th

S REDFIELD (Angora), S E fr Baltimore av to Angora, W of S 59th

S REESE, S fr 510 Cypress to De Lancey, 508 Lombard to South, Kater to S of Bainbridge, N & S fr 506 Catharine to Queen, & fr Carpenter to League, & fr Tree to Porter, W of S 5th

S ROSEWOOD, S fr 1412 Spruce to De Lancey, N fr Bainbridge, S fr Kater to Catharine, Tasker to Morris, Watkins to Mifflin, Snyder av to Ritner & fr Porter to Shunk, W of S Broad

S SARTAIN, S fr 1118 Locust to Manning, 1132 Rodman to South, Bainbridge to Catharine, Montrose to Hall, Moore to McKean, & fr Ritner to W Moyam'g av, W of S 11th

S SCHELL, S fr Ludlow to Ranstead, Chancellor to W of S 8th 816 Locust to Spruce, 834 South to Fitzwater, & N fr Montrose, W of S 8th

S SHEDWICK, S fr Reed to Gray's Ferry av, W of S 34th, & (W P), fr 3426 Market to Ludlow

S SHERIDAN, S fr 632 Fitzwater, 624 Catharine to Webster, 624 Wash'n av, N fr 613 Annin, & S fr Manton to 633 Wharton

S SMEDLEY, S fr 1610 Spruce to Pine, & fr 1618 Bainbridge to Fitzwater

S SPANGLER, N fr 3311 Wharton, & fr S fr Oakford to Reed, W of S 33d

S STANLEY, N fr Gray's Ferry av to Schuyl av, W of S 30th

S STILLMAN, N fr 2519 Christian

S SWANSON, S fr Lombard to 11 South, thence to Government av

S SYDENHAM, S fr 1514 Walnut to Locust, Waverly to Lombard, & fr Federal to r of 1514 Ellsworth

S TANEY, S fr Pine to Bainbridge, & fr Catharine to Christian, W of S 26th

S UBER, S fr Ranstead to Ludlow, & fr 1918 Pine to Lombard, W of S 19th

RICHARDSON & ROSS, 30th & Race Sts.

S VAN PELT, S fr Ludlow to Walnut, N & S fr Locust to Spruce, & fr Pine to Lombard, W of S 21st

S WARNOCK, S fr Walnut to Spruce, Bainbridge to Christian, N & S fr Wharton to Reed, Mifflin to McKean, & fr Wolf to Porter, W of S 10th

S WATER, S fr Market to Bainbridge, N fr 15 Fitzwater, N fr Beck, & fr 26 Christian to Government av, W of S Del av

S WATTS, S fr 1334 Walnut, Locust to Spruce, Cypress to Lombard, Fitzwater to Carpenter, Wharton to Titan, Reed to Watkins, Moore to Snyder av, Jackson to Wolf, & fr Ritner to W Moyam'g av, E of S Broad

S WENDLE, S fr 608 Locust

S WOODSTOCK, S fr Chancellor to 2011 Locust, Wharton to Reed, Dickinson to Tasker, & fr Mifflin to Snyder av, W of S 20th

S 2D, S fr 200 Market to Mifflin, & fr 150 Mifflin to Government av

S 3D, S fr 300 Market to bel Reed, & fr Mifflin to Government av

S 4TH, S fr 400 Market to Government av

S 5TH, S fr 500 Market to Government av

S 6TH, S fr 600 Market to Government av

S 7TH, S fr 700 Market to Walnut, & fr Irving to Government av

S 8TH, S fr 800 Market to Government av

S 9TH, S fr 900 Market to Government av

S 10TH, S fr 1000 Market to Government av

S 11TH, S fr 1100 Market to Reed, & fr 1525 Passy'k av to Government av

S 12TH, S fr 1200 Market to Government av

S 13TH, S fr 1300 Market to Government av

S 15TH, S fr 1500 Market to Passy'k av, thence S to Government av

S 16TH, S fr 1600 Market to Government av

S 17TH, S fr 1700 Market to Moore, & fr W Passy'k av to Government av

S 18TH, S fr 1800 Market to Government av

S 19TH, S fr 1900 Market to Mifflin, & fr Jackson to Government av

S 20TH, S fr 2000 Market to Government av

S 21ST, S fr 2100 Market to Mifflin, & fr Wolf to Government av

S 22D, S fr 2200 Market to McKean, & fr Jackson to Government av

S 23D, S fr 2300 Market to South, & fr Bainbridge to Federal

S 24TH, S fr 2400 Ludlow to Bainbridge, & fr Gray's Ferry av to Government av

S 25TH, S fr 2500 Locust to South & Gray's Ferry av, & fr Christian to Av 38 S to Government av

S 26TH, S fr 2600 Spruce to Bainbridge, 2536 Christian to Carpenter, & fr Gray's Ferry av & Carpenter to Av 38 S to Schuy'l av

S 27TH, S fr 2640 Lombard to Bainbridge, & fr Ellsworth to Av 39 S, & fr Av 42 S to Girard Pt

S 28TH, S fr Peltz to Schuy'l av

S 29TH, S fr Gray's Ferry av & Oakford to Schuy'l av

S 30TH, S fr Gray's Ferry av & Oakford to Schuy'l av, & (W P) S fr 3000 Market to Spruce

S 31ST, N & S fr Gray's Ferry av to Reed, & (W P), S fr 3100 Market to Spruce

S 32D, S fr Gray's Ferry av to Schuy'l av, & (W P), S fr Market to Chestnut, W of S 31st

S 33D, S fr Gray's Ferry av to Schuy'l av, & (W P), S fr 3300 Market to Spruce

S 34TH, S fr Schuy'l av to Schuy'l, & (W P), S fr 3400 Market to Schuy'l riv

S 35TH, S fr Gray's Ferry av to Schuy'l riv, & (W P), S fr 3500 Market to Locust

S 36TH, S fr Gray's Ferry av to Spruce, & fr Pine to Schuy'l riv, & (W P), S fr 3600 Market to Woodland av

S 37TH (W P), S fr 3700 Market to Woodland av

S 38TH (W P), S fr 3800 Market to Woodland av

S 39TH (W P), S fr 3900 Market to Woodland av

ASPHALTUM BLOCKS and TILES.

S 40TH (W P), S fr 4000 Market to Woodland av

S 41ST (W P), S fr 4100 Market to Woodland av

S 42D (W P), S fr 4200 Market to Schuy'l riv

S 43D (W P), S fr 4300 Market to Woodland av

S 44TH (W P), S fr 4400 Market to Kingsessing av

S 45TH (W P), S fr 4500 Market to Baltimore av, S E to Schuy'l riv

S 46TH (W P), S fr 4600 Market to Baltimore av, S E to Schuy'l riv

S 47TH (W P), S fr 4700 Market to Baltimore av, S E to Schuy'l riv

S 48TH (W P), S fr 4800 Market to Baltimore av, S E to Schuy'l riv

S 49TH (W P), S fr 4900 Market to Baltimore av, S E to Schuy'l riv

S 50TH (W P), S fr 5000 Market to Baltimore av, S E to Schuy'l riv

S 51ST (W P), S fr 5100 Market to Baltimore av, S E to Schuy'l riv

S 52D (W P), S fr 5200 Market to Baltimore av, S E to Schuy'l riv

S 53D (W P), S fr 5300 Market to Baltimore av, S E to Schuy'l riv

S 54TH (W P), S fr 5400 Market to Baltimore av, S E to Schuy'l riv

S 55TH (W P), S fr 5500 Market to Baltimore av, S E to Schuy'l riv

S 56TH (W P), S fr 5600 Market to Baltimore av, S E to Schuy'l riv

S 57TH (W P), S fr 5700 Market to Baltimore av, S E to Schuy'l riv

S 58TH (W P), S fr 5800 Market to Baltimore av, S E to Schuy'l riv

S 59TH (W P), S fr 5900 Market to Baltimore av, S E to Schuy'l riv

S 60TH (W P), S fr 6000 Market to Baltimore av, S E to Schuy'l riv

S 61ST (W P), S fr 6100 Market to Baltimore av, & S E fr Warrington av to Schuy'l riv

S 62D (W P), S E fr 6200 Market to Wharton, & S E fr Warrington av to Schuy'l riv

S 63D (W P), S fr 6300 Market to Federal, & S E fr Warrington av to Schuy'l riv

S 64TH (W P), S E fr Kingsessing av to Schuy'l riv

S 65TH (W P), S E fr Springfield av & Mt Moriah Cemetery to Schuy'l riv

S 66TH to S 90TH (W P), on city plan, S E fr Cobb's creek to Schuy'l riv

SOUTHAMPTON AV (C Hill), S W fr 8300 Gtn av, to Wiss av, S E of Union av (See also E Southampton av)

SOUTHAMPTON RD (Byberry), N W fr Bensalem pike to Cemetery la

SOWER'S CT, E fr 1415 Randolph

SPANGLER, S fr Wiccacoe av to Government av, W of S Del av (See also N & S Spangler—W P)

SPEILBERGER'S CT, E fr 1531 N Hancock

SPENCER AV, W fr Old York rd to N 18th, & (Gtn), fr N 20th to Stenton av, S of Godfrey av

SPENCER'S CT, S fr 2052 Lombard

SPOONER'S AV, W fr 1114 N American

SPRAGUE (Gtn), N fr Church la to E Wash'n la, W of Boyer, & (C Hill), N fr Abington av to Hartwell av, E of Gtn av

SPRING, W fr 206 N Front, 208 N 8th to N 11th, Madison to N Juniper, 214 N 15th to N 17th, N 21st to N 22d, & E fr N 23d

SPRING AL (Gtn), W fr 5100 Gtn av

SPRING GARDEN, W fr 520 N 6th to N 25th, & (W P), fr N 31st to N 42d

SPRING GARDEN RETREAT, N fr 1217 Spg Garden

SPRING HOUSE PIKE (C Hill), N fr Gtn av & Rex

SPRINGER (Gtn), N E fr 6665 Gtn av to Musgrove, S of Phil-Ellena

SPRINGER'S CT, S fr 116 Christian

SPRINGFIELD AV (C Hill), S W fr 7900 Gtn av to Wiss drive, N of Moreland av (See also E Springfield av)

SPRINGFIELD AV (W P), S W fr Baltimore av to Mt Moriah Cemetery, S of Warrington av

SPRUCE, W fr 300 S Del av to Schuy'l riv & (W P), fr S 34th & South to Cobb's creek

SPRUCE-MILL RD (C Hill), N W fr N 28th & Highland av to N 32d & Wiss creek

RICHARDSON & ROSS, 30th & Race Sts.

STAFFORD (Gtn), S E fr Baynton to Lena, S E of Chelten av & N E fr Morris to Wiss av, ab Chelten av

STAMPERS, W fr 418 S 2d to S 3d

STAMPERS LA, W fr Wiccacoe av to Stone House la, S of Shunk

STANLEY (See N & S Stanley)

STANTON (Falls), E fr 4201 Ridge av to G & N R R

STANWOOD (Fox Chase), S E fr Montg'y County line, S W of Solly

STARKEY (Eln), N E fr Pennypack to Lott, S E of Evans

STARR GARDEN, S 7th, Lombard to Rodman

STATE (W P), N fr Filbert to Barl·g, Warren to Willow, & fr Poplar to Englesfield, E of N 40th

STATE HOUSE ROW, S side of Chestnut, fr S 5th to S 6th

STATE RD (Tacony), W fr Levick to Cottman, S of Phila. & Trenton R R

STATION AL (Myk), E fr Cotton to Roxb, N of Cresson

STAUB (N Town), E fr 4155 Gtn av to Nice

STEARLEY'S CT, W fr 620 Galloway

STECK'S CT, W fr 914 Mascher

STEIMAN'S CT, E fr 1419 Randolph

STEINBERG (W P), W fr Conshohocken av to Windemere av

STEINER, N fr 929 Wallace to Melon

STEINRUCK AV, S fr 252 Oxford

STELLA, W fr N Hancock to Palethorp, N American to N 3d. & fr 2932 N 8th to N 11th, S of Indiana (See also E Stella)

STENTON AV (Gtn), N E fr Gtn av to Fisher's la, N of Crittenden

STENTON PARK (22d ward), N 16th to N 17th, Wyoming to Courtland

STERNER, W fr A to N Front, 2714 N 9th to N Hutchinson, & fr N 26th to N 28th, N of Lehigh av (See also E Sterner)

STEVENSON'S CT, E fr 917 S 5th

STEVENSON'S LA (Torresdale), S E fr Fkd av to P R R, S of Torresdale rd

STEWART, W fr N 21st to N 27th & (W P), fr N 54th to N 55th, S of Jefferson

STILES, W fr 1210 Cadwallader to Gtn av, 1232 N 11th to N 19th, 1248 N 26th to N 31st & (W P), N W fr N 42d to Belmont av, 4901 Girard av to N 52d, W fr Daggett, S of Haverford, & E fr N 66th

STILES (Fkd), N fr Ashland to Fkd av, S of Melrose

STILLMAN (See N & S Stillman)

STOCK EXCHANGE PL, W fr S 3d to Oriana, S of Chestnut

STOKLEY, N fr Hunting Park av, E of Fox

STOLL'S CT, E fr 1429 Gtn av

STONE HOUSE LA, S E fr Old 2d, E to Jones' la, S of Ritner

STOUTON, N E fr Hart la to E Cambria, & fr E Clearfield to Clementine, W of Jasper

STRAHLE (Fox Chase), N W fr H to Pine rd, E of Hoffnagle

STRATTON'S CT, E fr 1315 N Hancock

STRAUSS' CT, W fr 802 S 6th

STRAWBERRY, S fr 214 Market to Chestnut

STREEPER (Roxb), W fr Ridge av, N of Manatawna rd

STREEPER'S CT, E fr 1003 Oriana

STURTEVANT (W P), W fr S 42d to 53d, S of Market

SUFFOLK AV (W P), S W fr Gibson av to Island rd, bel S 70th

SULLIVAN (C Hill), W fr Stenton av to Evergreen av, N of Sprague & fr C Hill av to County line, Reading pike, E of Gtn av

SUMAC, N fr Cumberland to Huntingdon, & (Wiss), N E fr Ridge av to Rochelle av, S W of Osborn

SUMMER, W fr 228 N Front, E fr 231 N 2d, W fr 232 N 5th to N 6th, 230 N 8th to N Darien, 213 N Clifton, N 12th to N 13th, 242 N 15th to N 18th, N 20th to N 23d, W fr N Bonsall & (W P) N 32d to Natrona, N 55th to N 58th & fr Gross to N 64th, S of Vine

SUMMERFIELD PL, N fr 329 Green

SHEET ASPHALT PAVING of all kinds.

SUMMERS PL (W P), E fr 5 S 37th
SUMMIT (C Hill), W fr 8700 Gtn av, N of Evergreen av, & fr Bethlehem pike to Stenton av, & (Roxb), N E of Shawmont, fr Ridge av to Wiss, Park drive
SUN CT, S fr 916 Ogden
SUNDGARD, N W fr E Allegheny av, W of H
SUNNYSIDE (Falls), S W fr N 34th to Cresson, N of Bowman
SUNSET (C Hill), W fr N 30th n Stenton av, W of Hildeburn
SUSQUEHANNA (Fox Chase)
SUSQUEHANNA AV, W fr 2152 N Front to N 22d, N 26th to N 33d & (W P) N W fr George's av to N 57th (See also E Susq'ana av)
SUTTON, W fr 1432 N 5th to N Randolph
SWAIN, W fr 712 N 15th to Folsom, N 25th to N Taney, & fr N 27th to N 28th
SWANSON (See N & S Swanson)
SWANSON'S CT, W fr 842 S Swanson
SWANWICK, S fr 606 Sansom to Walnut
SWARTZ PL, S fr 244 Fulton to Catharine
SYDENHAM (See N & S Sydenham)
SYLVAN (W P), W fr N 37th to N 38th, S of Poplar

T.

TABOR RD (Olney), E fr Old York rd, S of Chew
TACKAWANNA (Tac & Hbg), N E fr Tyson to Princeton, & fr Benner to Robbins, N W of Erdrick
TACKAWANNA (Fkd), N fr 151 Church to Harrison
TACOMA (Gtn), N fr Seymour to Manheim, Coulter to Winona av, & fr Price to Rittenhouse, W of Wayne
TACONY (Fkd), S E fr Paul to Lewis, thence N E to State rd, E of P R R
TAGGERT, N fr E Norris to E Dauphin, E of Cedar
TANEY (See N & S Taney)
TASKER, W fr Del riv to Schuy'l riv, 1600 S
TAYLOR, N fr Aspen to Poplar, N College av to Thompson & fr Montg'y av to N of Berks, W of N 24th

TAYLOR'S CT, E fr 721 S 3d
TERRACE (Myk & Wiss), S E fr Levering to Ridge av, S W of Myk av
TEST'S AV, E fr 1141 Dunton
THAYER (N Town), W fr N 8th to Goodman, S of Ontario (See also E Thayer)
THEWLIS CT (Gtn), N fr 303 Penn
THOLE (W P), W fr S 57th to County line, S of Baltimore av
THOMAS AV (W P), S W fr S 53d, & Baltimore av to Cobb's creek
THOMPSON, W fr 1300 Fkd av to Ridge av, N 22d to N 33d, & (W P), N W fr N 41st to Belmont av, S of Parkside av, & fr Lancaster av & N 49th to Haverford, thence to N 63d, N of Girard av (See also E Thompson)
THOMPSON PL, S fr 128 Race
THOMPSON'S CT, N fr 405 Cherry
THORN'S CT, N fr 1111 Melon
THORNTON RD (Byberry)
THORP'S LA (C Hill), W fr County line to Roxb, N of Sunset av
THORP'S LA (Gtn), E fr Wister, bel Chew
TIBBIN (Roxb), N E fr Fountain to Lemonte, N E of Silverwood
TILDEN PL, W fr 546 Randolph
TILGHMAN, N E fr 1723 N 2d to N Hancock
TILLER'S CT, E fr 219 S Sydenham
TILTON, N fr 2711 E Cumberland to E Huntingdon, S & N fr 2715 Neff to E Westmoreland, & fr Albert to E Venango, N W of Salmon, & (Bdg), fr Bucklus to Ash, E of Edgemont
TINICUM AV (P'ville), S fr S 86th to S 90th, N of Laycock av
TIOGA, W fr 3500 N Front to N Town la (See also E Tioga)
TITAN, W fr 1124 S Front to S Hancock, S Philip to S American, 1226 S 3d to S 6th, 1230 S 11th to S Iseminger, W fr S Watts, r 1325 Wharton, & fr S 16th to S 23d, S of Federal
TITUS (Tacony), N W fr State rd to P R R, N of Longshore
TOLBERT (Bln), S E fr Meeting House rd to Starkey, S of Carwithen
TOMLINSON (Bln), E fr Pennypack to Lott, N of Banes

RICHARDSON & ROSS, 30th & Race Sts.

TORONTO, W fr N Broad to N 15th, & fr N 20th to N 23d, N of Indiana (See also E Toronto)

TORRESDALE AV (Fkd), N E fr Tacony rd & Orchard to Wissino, N of Edmund

TOWER (Myk), N W fr Jamestown to Levering, S W of Terrace

TOWNSHIP LINE RD (Roxb), E fr Mechanic to Wiss av

TOWNSHIP LINE RD (Tacony), S E fr Bristol pike to Del riv, N of St Vincent av

TREE, W fr Del riv to S 13th, bel Jackson

TRENT PL, r 618 Weaver

TRENTON AV, N E fr E Norris to E Lehigh av, & fr Butler to E Erie av, E of N Front

TRENTON AV (Fkd), N E fr Vandike, E of Paul

TRINITY (W P), S W fr 1010 S 48th to S 49th, & fr S 59th to S 60th, N W of Chester av

TRINITY PL, S fr 222 Catharine

TRIPPLE (Roxb), N W fr McFadden, N E of Lilly

TROTTERS AL, W fr 34 S 2d to Strawberry

TRYON, W fr 504 S 21st to S 22d

TUCKER, W fr 2623 N 12th to N 13th, & fr N 15th to N 16th (See also E Tucker)

TUCKER (Fkd), S E fr Foulkrod to Fkd creek, E of Margaret

TULIP, N fr 1539 E Palmer to Fkd creek, W of Memphis

TULIP (Fkd), N E fr Fkd creek to Duncan, S E of Janney, & (Tacony), fr Rawle to Township line rd, & (Wissino), N E fr Van Kirk to Grant, N W of Keystone

TULL'S CT (Gtn), S E fr Rittenhouse, S W of Gtn av

TULLY'S CT, E fr 1529 Cadwallader

TULPEHOCKEN (Gtn), W fr 6200 Gtn av to Pulaski av, S E of Wash'n av (See also E Tulpehocken

TURNER, W fr N Front to N 2d, Randolph to N 6th, N 19th to N 21st, N 22d to N 26th, & fr N Patton to N 35d, S of Columbia av

TUSCANY, N fr Juniata, E of N Front

TUSCULUM, N W fr Garnet, parallel to Reading R R, & N E thereof

TWADDELL'S CT, N fr 1823 Ludlow

TWELVE FOOT AL, S fr 510 Kater to Bainbridge

TYSON (Tacony), S E fr Bustleton pike to State rd, S W of Princeton

U.

UBER (See N & S Uber)

ULLMER (Roxb), W fr Ridge av, N of Parker's av

ULRICH AV, W fr 1314 N 2d to Cadwallader

UMBRIA (Myk), N W fr Main to Domino la, & fr Leverington av bel Wigard

UMSTEAD'S ROW (Wiss), N fr Rittenhouse, W of Wiss av

UNDERHILL (Gtn), N W fr Haines S W of Chew

UNION (W P), fr Sloan to Warren, W of N 39th, N fr Haverford to P R R & fr Poplar to Cambridge, W of N 39th

UNION AV (C Hill), S W fr 8400 Gtn av, S E of Highland av to N 30th (See also E Union av)

UNION CT, S of 910 Wood

UNION PL, N fr 2431 Noble

UNITY (Fkd), W fr Walnut la to Adams N of Church

UNITY CT, S fr 718 Addison

UNIVERSITY (W P), W fr S 30th, S of Woodland av

UNRUH (Tacony), W fr Del riv, S of Knorr

UPLAND (W P), S fr S 47th to S 48th, S 50th to S 51st, S 60th to S 61st, S 66th to S 69th, S W fr S 70th to S 72d & Kingsessing av

UPSAL (Gtn), S W fr 6500 Gtn av to Wiss av, S of Sharpnack (See also E Upsal)

UPSHUR AV, E fr 325 Mascher

URBANNA, W fr N Capitol to 7 N 21st

UTAH (Gtn), N fr 31 Maplewood av

UTICA PL, W fr 416 S Hutchinson

V.

VALLEY (Fkd), N E fr Margaret to Pratt, S E of Tackawanna

VALLEY CT, E fr 105 N Franklin

VANCE (P'ville), S fr S 86th, E of Mornen av

ASPHALTUM BLOCKS and TILES.

VANDIKE (Fkd), E fr Fkd av to Orchard (Tacony), S fr Cottman to Unruh, W of Hegerman & (Hbg) fr Decatur to Rhawn, N W of Hegerman

VANHORN, W fr 1326 N Hancock to 1073 Gtn av

VANKIRK (Fkd), E fr G, S of Comly, & (Wissino), N W fr P R R, N of Dark Run la

VAN PELT (See N & S Van Pelt)

VASSAR (Wiss), N E fr Cresson to Ridge av, S E of Dawson

VENANGO, W fr Ktn av to N Town la, N of Tioga, 3600 N (See also E Venango)

VERBENA AV (Oak la sta), E fr Oak la, ab N P R R

VERNON PARK (22d ward), N of Chelten av, bet Gtn av & Green

VERREE RD (Fox Chase), W fr Welsh rd to 2d st pike

VICARIS (Wiss), N W fr Sumac to Lauriston, E of Righter

VICI, E fr Fkd av to Coral, N of Wheatsheaf la

VICKER'S CT, N fr 1711 Ludlow

VICTORIA, E fr 3619 Gtn av, & W fr N Smedley to N 17th, N of Tioga (See also E Victoria)

VIENNA, N W fr N Del av to Fkd av, N of E. Columbia av

VINCENT (Wiss), S E fr Adams, E of Myk av

VINE, W fr 300 N Del av to Schuy'l riv, & (W P), fr N 52d & Haverford to County line

VINEYARD, S W fr Ridge av to N 19th, S of Poplar

VINTAGE AV (W P), S W fr S 34th to University, S of Pine

VIOLA (W P), W fr N 41st to N 53d, N of Columbia av

VOGDES (W P), N W fr Market to Vine, W of N 55th

W.

WADSWORTH (Gtn), E fr Boyer to City line, N W of Mt Airy av

WAGNER'S CT, W fr 646 N 7th

WAKEFIELD (Gtn), N fr Fisher's la to Coulter, E of Gtn av, & fr 128 Price to Rittenhouse, N of Lena

WAKELING (Fkd), W fr 5000 Willow to Mercer, N of Harrison

WALDEN, W fr 48 N 21st to N 22d & (W P), E fr 57 N 38th to Cuthbert, & W fr 56 N 38th to Saunders, S of Powelton av

WALKER, N E fr Wakeling to Mt Sinai Cemetery, thence N W fr Dark Run la, W of Cottage to Hbg

WALLACE, W fr 622 N 4th to N 5th, N 7th to N 25th, N of Mt Vernon, & (W P) fr P R R & N 31st to N 48th, N of Haverford, & fr N 48th to N 49th, S of Fairmount av

WALLS CT, E fr 535 N 24th

WALN (Fkd), S fr 126 Oxford to Chew

WALN CT (Fkd), r 4416 Waln

WALNUT, W fr 200 S Del av to Schuy'l riv, & (W P), fr Schuy'l riv to Cobb's creek at S 64th to Del County line

WALNUT LA (Gtn), S W fr 6100 Gtn av to Wiss av, S E of Tulpehocken (See also E Walnut la)

WALNUT LA (Myk & Roxb), N E fr 4104 Main to Wissahickon av N W of Kingsley

WALNUT PL, S fr 316 Walnut to Willings al

WALTER, W fr 1210 N 12th to N Watts, N Carlisle to N 18th, & fr N 27th to N 30th, N of Girard av (See also E Walter)

WALTON AV (W P), W fr 630 S 48th to S 49th

WANAMAKER (W P), N fr Market, W of N 58th, & fr Media to Lansdowne av

WARD'S RETREAT, S fr 1232 Cambridge

WARFIELD, S fr Wharton, W of S 34th

WARNOCK (See N & S Warnock)

WARREN (W P), N W fr N 34th & Filbert to N 38th, E & W fr N 39th to N 40th, Ludwig to N 42d, & fr N 50th to Lansdowne av, S of Lancaster av

WARRINGTON AV (W P), S W fr Baltimore av, & S 47th to S 60th, S of Florence av

WASHINGTON AV, W fr 1100 S Del av to Gray's Ferry av

WASHINGTON CT, N fr 643 Lombard

WASHINGTON LA (Gtn); S W fr 6300 Gtn av to Wiss av, N W of Tulpehocken (See also E Wash'n la)

RICHARDSON & ROSS, 30th & Race Sts.

WASHINGTON LA (Myk), N fr Park line to Wiss av
WASHINGTON SQ., S fr Walnut to Irving, S 6th to S Franklin
WATER (See N & S Water)
WATER (Olney), N fr Somerville to Clarkson, E of N Front
WATERLOO, N fr Poplar, W of N Front, & 137 Jefferson, Columbia av to Montg'y av, Berks to Hewson, Diamond to Fontain, & fr Colona to P & R Rw
WATERVIEW PARK (22d ward), Price, Haines & Underhill & O Hill, branch of P & R Rw
WATKINS, W fr S Front to Moyam'g av, 1712 S 4th to S 12th, 1718 S 17th to S 18th, & fr S 19th to Pt Breeze av, S of Morris
WATTS (See N & S Watts)
WAVERLY, W fr 404 S 6th, S Hutchinson to S Juniper, S Carlisle to S 21st, E fr S Van Pelt, & fr S 23d to S 26th, S of Pine, & (W P), fr S 43d to S 54th, & fr S 59th to S 62d, S of Pine
WAYNE (N Town & Gtn), N W fr Hunting Park av & N 15th to Allen's la, N E of Pulaski av
WAYNE TER (Gtn), W fr 4360 Gtn av
WEAVER (Gtn), N E fr Chelten av to Limekiln turnpike, N W of Upsal
WEAVER AV, E fr 1539 Gtn av to Cadwallader
WEBB, N fr 2669 E Cumberland to E Lehigh av, & fr Albert to Reading R R Division to E Allegheny av, & fr Madison to E Ontario, E of E Thompson
WEBSTER, W fr 808 Passy'k av to S 7th, S 11th to S Broad, S Rosewood to S Mole, 810 S 16th, W fr opp 813 S 17th to S 22d, & fr opp S Stillman to Schuyl av S of Catharine
WEIGHTMAN, S fr 2226 Montg'y av, & fr Ridge av, Park drive
WEIKEL, N E fr 2253 Auburn to William, & fr Oakdale to E Erie av, W of Tulip
WELCOME (P'ville), S E fr Woodland av & S 71st to P W & B R R, thence fr S 90th to Gibson av, & E to Bartram av
WILKER'S AV, S fr 2022 Herman

WELSH RD (Bln), S W fr Montg'y County line to Charles (Hbg), E of Rhawn
WENDLE (See N & S Wendle)
WENDOVER (Myk), S W fr 4114 Myk av to Terrace, & N E fr Apple to Tower ab Walnut la
WENSLEY, W fr N 20th to N 23d, S of Ontario (See also E Wensley)
W LOGAN SQ (N 19th), Race to Vine
W MOYAMENSING AV, S W fr S 5th, & Jackson to Penrose av, bel Snyder av
W PASSYUNK AV, W fr S Broad & McKean to Schuy'l riv
W RITTENHOUSE SQ (S 19th), Walnut to Rittenhouse sq
W SHIPPEN PL, N fr 829 Bainbridge
WESTERN AV, W fr 222 N 15th
WESTFORD AV, S fr 808 Noble
WESTMINSTER AV (W P), W fr N 39th, N of Ogden to City av
WESTMONT, W fr 2138 N Marshall to N 7th, & fr 2120 N 29th to N 30th, & fr N 31st to N 32d, N of Diamond
WESTMORE PL, E fr 515 N 2d
WESTMORELAND, W fr 3300 Fkd av to N Town la, thence fr R R to Abbotsford av, 3300 N. (See also E Westmoreland)
WESTVIEW AV (Gtn), S W fr 6700 Gtn av, N W of Phil-Ellena
WETHERILL (Wiss), S fr Sumac to Fairmount Park, W of Rochelle av
WEYMOUTH, N fr 715 D Clearfield to E Allegheny av, E of F
WHARF (Fkd), S E fr Orchard to Fkd creek, S of Pierce
WHARTMAN (Roxb), S fr Domino la, W of Wood
WHARTON, W fr 1300 S Front, S 37th & (W P) fr Baltimore av to Cobb's creek
WHARTON SQ, S 12th to S 13th, Wharton to Reed
WHEATSHEAF LA, N W fr Del av to Old Front Street rd, N E of Butler
WHEELOCK'S PL, N fr 1331 Potts to Fairmount av
WHITBY AV (W P), S W fr 5116 Baltimore av to Cobb's creek, S of Thomas av
WHITE'S CT, E fr 1533 N Front

6

SHEET ASPHALT PAVING of all kinds.

WHITE'S CT, S fr 1326 Kater

WHITEBREAD PL, S fr 122 Christian

WHITEHEAD'S CT, W fr 736 S 4th

WHITMER'S AL, W fr 358 N Orianna to N 4th

WHYTE'S PL, S fr 1236 South

WICCACOE AV, S E fr Swanson to Del riv, S of Snyder av

WICCACOE PARK (3d ward), Catharine to Queen, Wiccacoe to S Lawrence

WIEHLE (Falls), N fr Sunnyside to P & R Rw, W of N 35th

WIGARD AV (Roxb), E fr Shawmont St to N E of Shawmont av, S E of Williams av

WILCOX, W fr 534 N 19th to N 20th, & fr 530 N 21st to N 22d & to Hermitage

WILDE (Myk), N W fr Green la to Hermitage, E of Ritchie

WILDER, W fr Moyam'g av to Dickinson, E & W fr 1426 S 4th to S 10th, N W fr Dickinson to S 13th, 1426 S 18th to S 21st & fr S 22d to S 24th

WILDEY, W fr Fkd av to 945 N 4th. (See also E Wildey)

WILLARD, W fr N 5th to 3253 N 6th & fr 3232 N 19th to N 20th, N of Westmoreland (See also E. Willard)

WILLETTS RD (Hbg), N W fr Bristol turnpike to Hbg or Welsh rd, Del township line

WILLIAM, W fr 2828 N 12th to N 13th, S of Cambria (See also E William)

WILLIAMS AL, S fr 528 Bainbridge to Kenilworth

WILLIAMS AV (Gtn), N W fr Limekiln pk to Montg'y County line, N of Thouron

WILLINGS AL, W fr 224 S 3d to S 4th

WILLINGTON, N fr 1619 Master to Berks

WILLOW, W fr Del av to N 10th, N of Callowhill

WILLOW (Fkd), N E fr Meadow to Bridge, N W of Hawthorne

WILLOW (Hbg), E fr Decatur, N of Bristol turnpike

WILLOW (W P), W fr State to Union, N of Baring

WILLOW GROVE AV (C Hill) S W fr 8000 Gtn av to N 36th, N W of Springfield av (See also E Willow Grove av)

WILLOWS AV (W P), S W fr S 50th & Baltimore av to Cobb's creek, S E of Whitby av

WILMOT (Fkd), N E fr Almond to Fkd creek

WILSON (Gtn), S fr 424 Haines

WILT, W fr 1822 N Howard to N Mascher, 1818 N 6th to N Marshall, 1816 Gratz to N Ub r, & fr 1818 N 31st to N 32d (See also E Wilt)

WILTBANK'S CT, r 3 De Gray

WILTON (W P), N fr Warren to Media, & fr Jefferson to Columbia av, W of N 52d

WINDEMERE AV (W P), bet Falls rd & Overbrook, S of P & R Rw, thence S W & S E to Crestline av

WINDSOR (W P), W fr S 47th to S 50th, ab Springfield av

WINGATE (Hbg), S W fr Ashburner's la, N W of Trenton R R

WINGOHOCKING (Fkd), N E fr Adams to 1332 Sellers

WINGOHOCKING (Gtn), S W fr Gtn av to Greene

WINONA (Gtn), S W fr 5432 Wayne to a point N E of Laurens, N W of Coulter

WINTER, W fr 248 N 8th, N 9th to N Juniper, N 15th to beyond N 17th, N Opal to W of N Van Pelt, & fr N Bonsall to N 24th, & (W P), W fr 222 N 32d to Natrona, S of Powelton av

WINTER'S CT, S fr 1234 Summer

WINTON, W fr 2134 S 3d & fr 2130 S 5th to S 12th

WIOTA (W P), N fr 4021 Market to Spg Garden, Wallace to Aspen, & fr Parrish to Westminster av, W of N 40th

WISDOM AL (Gtn), W fr 6218 Gtn av

WISE'S MILL RD (Roxb), S W fr Wiss av, S of Summit av

WISHART, W fr N 13th to Park av, & W fr N 17th, N of Clearfield (See also E Wishart)

WISHART'S CT, W fr 704 Beach

WISLER AV, E fr 1747 N 2d

WISSAHICKON AV, N W fr N 22d & Tioga to Wiss creek

RICHARDSON & ROSS, 30th & Race Sts.

WISSINOMING (Tacony), N E fr Knorr to County line, S E of Tacony

WISTARIA (Bln), N E fr Fulmer to Lott, S of Bln pike

WISTER (Gtn), E fr 5031 Gtn av to G, & N R R, S E of Collom & S W fr Portico, S of Manheim

WISTER PL (Gtn), r of 30 Wister

WITTEE, N W fr E Auburn to E Cambria, & fr Ann to E Erie av, E of Trenton av

WOLF, W fr Del riv to Schuy'l riv, 2300 S

WOLF'S CT, S fr 314 Fitzwater

WOLF PL, E fr 508 N American

WOLPER'S CT, E fr 161 N 23d

WOLSTENHOLME AV (Fkd), N W fr Cambridge to Stiles, S of Orthodox

WOMRATH (Fkd), E fr Torresdale av to Mercer, S of Ruan

WOMRATH PARK (23d ward), Ktn av, Fkd av & Adams

WOMRATH PL, N fr 235 Monroe

WONDERLY PL, N fr 149 Wildey

WOOD, W fr 308 Mascher to N 24th, N of Vine

WOOD (W P), N W fr N 32d to Natrona, N of Race

WOODBINE AV (W P), N E fr N 48th, S of Drexel rd & N W fr N 63d

WOODLAND AV (W P), S W fr Market & S 31st to Cobb's creek

WOODLAND TER (W P), S fr Baltimore av to Woodland av, W of S 40th

WOODLAWN (Gtn), N E fr 5605 Gtn av & fr Morton to Anderson, S E of Chelten av

WOODSTOCK (See N & S Woodstock

WOODSTOCK (Gtn), N fr Church la to Godfrey av, W of N 21st

WOODVALE (Wiss) (was Kalos), N E fr 3717 Ridge av to Righter, N W of Sumac

WOODVILLE PL, N fr 1723 Ransted

WORKMAN'S PL, S fr 116 Pemberton

WORRELL (Fkd), S E fr 4105 Fkd av to Tacony

WORTH (Fkd), N E fr Oxford to Tucker, S of Edgmont

WORTHINGTON RD (Byberry), S W fr Southampton rd to Berry rd

WREN (Hbg), N E fr William to Holmesburg, E of Montague

WRIGHT (Myk), N E fr P & R Rw to Smick, N of Levering

WYALUSING (W P), W fr N 38th to N 58th & Haverford, N of Westminster av

WYLIE, S W fr 1654 Ridge av to N 19th

WYNNFIELD AV (W P) N E fr N Alden, & Overbrook av to Caroline av

WYOMING (Gtn), N E fr Pulaski av to Gtn av, thence S E fr 4687 Gtn av to P N of Courtland

WYOMING AV (Feltonville)

X.

XENOPHON AV (W P), W fr N 60th, N of Haverford

Y.

YOCUM (P'ville), W fr Melville to S 46th, 1306 Lincoln sq to S 49th bel Kingsessing av, S 53d to S 56th, & Gray's la, S 66th to S 69th, & fr S 70th to S 73d, N of Woodland av

YORICK PL (Fkd), E fr Fkd av, N of Ruan

YORK, W fr 2400 N Front to N 34th. (See also E York)

YORK AV, N W fr N 4th & Wood to 549 N 5th

YORK PL, E fr 875 N 5th

YORK RD, N W fr 3225 Gtn av, n Rising Sun la, to County line

YOUNG'S AL, S fr 152 Pegg to Willow, & W fr 426 Mascher

YUNGLING, W fr N 33d, N of York

Z.

ZAUN'S CT, W fr 706 Bodine

ZELLS PL (Torresdale)

ZERELDA (Gtn), S W fr Wayne to Pulaski av, N W of Berkley

ZIMMER (P'ville), S fr Powers la, E of Buist av

STREET NUMBERS.

NORTH.

)m-	1500 Jefferson.
	1600 Oxford.
	1700 Columbia Ave.
:h.	1800 Montgomery Ave.
	1900 Berks.
)w,	2000 Norris.
tta.	2100 Diamond.
ing	2200 Susquehanna Ave.
	2300 Dauphin.
on,	2400 York.
1.	2500 Cumberland.
.ve.	2600 Huntingdon.
Og-	2700 Lehigh Ave.
	2800 Somerset.
.av-	2900 Cambria.
	3000 Indiana.
5.	3100 Clearfield.
rt.	3200 Allegheny Ave.
d.	3300 Westmoreland.

3400 Ontario.
3500 Tioga.
3600 Venango.
3700 Erie Ave.
3800 Butler.
3900 Pike.
4000 Luzerne.
4100 Roxborough.
4200 Juniata.
4300 Bristol.
4400 Cayuga.
4500 Wingohocking.
4600 Courtland.
4700 Wyoming Ave.
4800 Loudon.
4900 Rockland.
5000 Ruscomb.
5100 Lindley, Wynne.

SOUTH.

[er-	1500 Dickinson, Green-
	wich.
)m,	1600 Tasker, Sylvester.
	1700 Morris, Watkins.
	1800 Moore, Siegel.
	1900 Mifflin.
	2000 McKean.
.	2100 Snyder Ave.
	2200 Jackson.
)oe,	2300 Wolf.
ian	2400 Ritner.
.	2500 Porter.
:t.	2600 Shunk.
	2700 Oregon Ave.
lls-	2800 Johnston.
	2900 Bigler.
	3000 Pollock.
	3100 Packer.
	3200 Curtin.

3300 Geary.		
3400 Hartranft.		
3500 Hoyt.		
Avenue 36 South.		
"	37	"
"	38	"
"	39	"
"	40	"
"	41	"
"	42	"
"	43	"
"	44	"
"	45	"
Government Ave.		
Schuylkill Ave.		
League Island.		

SUBURBS.

	Fox Chase. 35th ward.
	Frankford. 23d ward.
	Franklinville. 33d ward.
.rd.	Germantown. 22d ward.
	Haddington. 34th ward.
d.	Hestonville. 34th ward.
.	Holmesburg. 35th ward.
	Lawndale. 22d ward.
	Manayunk. 21st ward.
.rd.	Mantua. 34th ward.
.rd.	McCartersville. 22d ward.
d.	Mechanicsville. 23d ward.
d.	Milestown. 22d ward.
.rd.	Nicetown. 33d ward.
	Oak Lane Sta., P. R. R.
8th	22d ward.
	Olney. 22d ward.
.	Overbrook. 34th ward.
d.	Paschalville. 27th ward.

Pelham, 22d ward.
Pittville. 22d ward.
Rising Sun. 33d ward.
Rittenhouseville. 21st ward.
Rowlandville. 22d ward.
Roxborough. 21st ward.
Somerton. 35th ward.
Somerville. 22d ward.
Sunnycliff. 21st ward.
Tacony. 35th ward.
Tioga. 28th ward.
Torresdale. 35th ward.
Unionville. 22d ward.
Verree's Mills. 35th ward.
Volunteer Town. 35th wd.
Whitehall. 23d ward.
Wissahickon. 21st ward.
Wissinoming. 35th ward.

www.ingramcontent.com/pod-product-compliance
Lightning Source LLC
Chambersburg PA
CBHW020314090426

42735CB00009B/1338